BIBLICAL HEBREW

Biblical Hebrew

A BEGINNER'S MANUAL

by

Harvey E. Finley, Ph.D.

Professor of Old Testament
Nazarene Theological Seminary

and

Charles D. Isbell, Ph.D.

Assistant Professor of Classics
University of Massachusetts, Amherst

Beacon Hill Press of Kansas City

Kansas City, Missouri

Copyright, 1975

Beacon Hill Press of Kansas City

Revised with Charts, 1979

ISBN: 0-8341-0350-8

Printed in the United States of America

PREFACE

This book began in 1968 as a project to make the study of Hebrew a more vital part of the curriculum at Nazarene Theological Seminary in Kansas City, Missouri. Since that time, the materials have evolved in about four stages, each draft more polished than the last and each one heavily indebted to the students who used, criticized and learned from it.

Accordingly, the authors wish to thank their many students, both at Nazarene Theological Seminary and at the University of Massachusetts, Amherst, for their contributions to the finished product as well as for the encouragement and stimulation which good students always provide for their teachers.

Special appreciation is expressed to Mr. Kenneth W. Wesche, student at Nazarene Theological Seminary, who gave most helpful assistance in the typing and completing of other aspects of this revision.

HARVEY E. FINLEY, PH.D.

CHARLES D. ISBELL, PH.D.

NTS, 1979

TO THE TEACHER

This book is designed as an introduction to Biblical Hebrew for the purpose of enabling one to learn to read the earlier Scriptures in their original language, except the Aramaic passages. An average class should complete this book in approximately a semester and a half, assuming about two class days are spent on each lesson.

A student will learn the basic elements of grammar, syntax, and word inflection in completing this text. One will have become familiar with approximately 500 vocabulary words, and have read chapters 22-27 (226 verses!) of Genesis. The Genesis readings are an essential element in the plan of this book. In addition to the standard contrived sentences, the student begins to read the Biblical text by the end of Lesson Four. This not only avoids the trap of forcing students to read countless sentences which simply do not occur in the Bible. It also tends to create interest and excitement because one begins early to use Hebrew in a meaningful way.

Each "reading-exercise" passage from Genesis is accompanied by notes. These are rather extensive at first, and they are intended to help the student translate verb forms or constructions not yet explained in a lesson. You as teacher must recognize with this approach a student cannot be expected to translate entirely on his own, certainly not early in the course. You may wish to suggest the use of a recent modern translation, such as the Revised Standard Version, New American Standard Bible, or New International Bible, along with the notes provided in this text. Or, you may wish to have students obtain a text with full translation to be used for the first time the class works through chapters 22-26. However, you will want to take your class through these chapters again after you have studied all the basic aspects of grammar completing the Strong and Weak verbs (Lesson 33). It is at this time you should insist that students must dispense with translation or inter-linear helps and translate on the basis of their knowledge of the language.

Further, review lists of vocabulary and charts of various parts of the grammar are located throughout the text. These should be strategic review times for your class; it is well to insist on memorization of these vocabulary lists and grammar review charts at the point at which they are located in the text.

A word about exercises. The authors have not found it useful to force first-year students to compose sentences in Hebrew which will be neither correct nor "correct-able".

English to Hebrew composition is helpful, for third or
fourth year students! Before that stage, a student's time
may be better spent.

There is a tape made specifically to accompany this
book. It contains audio materials which will augment the
student's knowledge gained visually and may be used in a
variety of ways, again depending upon the needs of a class
and its teacher. The tape may be ordered from Beacon Hill
Press in Kansas City, Missouri.

הו, עוד דבר. במבוא לתלמידים אומרים שמורים לעברית
בכל העולם מפורסמים לטוב לב, סבלנות, ונדיבות. אל תשכח את
השם הטוב שלנו.

TO THE STUDENT

Hebrew is a member of the Semitic language family,
and is strikingly different from English and other Indo-
European languages. Nevertheless, it has a significant
relationship with them because it was from an old Semitic
alphabet that the Indo-European alphabet derived. Several
of the main peculiarities of Hebrew are: (a) it is written
from right to left, involving reversal of pagination; (b)
it is mainly a consonantal language in its written forms;
(c) its two main parts of speech are the verb and the noun
in that order and these consist, for the most part, in triliteral roots; (d) it is a morphologically limited language
for it does not have case endings for nouns or modal endings
for verbs.

The Hebrew found in the Bible is called "Classical
Hebrew" to distinguish it from the Hebrew of early inscript-
ional materials and from post-biblical and modern Hebrew.
Biblical Hebrew is not entirely new to you, for you have
no doubt pronounced many Hebrew words while reading aloud
the various personal and place names found in the English
Old Testament. These are mainly transliterations from the
Hebrew. But Hebrew is different, and you will need to ad-
just your thinking about languages if you want to master any
Semitic tongue, including Hebrew.

Learning Hebrew Can Be Exciting!

The experience of the authors, whose lot it has been to attempt the mastery of many languages, has taught them the following principles which should be followed by every student who uses this book:

1. Do not fall behind silently. If you do not have a satisfactory grasp of what is happening in a session, it is important that you ask for an explanation from your instructor. The chances are good that several others in the class need to hear the same question answered that puzzles you. Remember that Hebrew instructors around the world are known for their kindness, patience, and generosity. Your instructor is heir to this reputation, and you ought never to hesitate in asking for his help when you need it.

2. Take everything step by step. Do not make the common mistake of failing to read an explanation carefully or neglecting to learn well a new vocabulary list before you start to do an exercise.

3. Make it a standard practice to read everything aloud. It is smart to copy the pronunciation of the tape which accompanies this book or to copy the pronunciation of your instructor as closely as you can. But even when you are studying alone, you should read and reread each lesson several times aloud.

4. Understand from the beginning that language is a subject which requires time, particularly early in a year or semester. There is no settled standard about the exact amount of time which will unfailingly produce that elusive "A". Be prepared to spend as much time as YOU need, regardless of how little or how much someone else may claim to be spending.

5. Adopt and exploit the truth that _repetitio est mater studiorum_. If you study Hebrew one hour per day, six days per week, the total time invested might be adequate, but the impact on the brain unsatisfactory. But if you study Hebrew INTENSIVELY WITH NO DISTRACTIONS three times daily, 20 minutes per session, your brain will be attacked by Demon Grammar on twenty-one (three class sessions!) separate occasions each week. Few brains can withstand such an assault, and some knowledge of Hebrew will certainly result. Note that in this formula the biblical six-day working week is assumed.

6. Begin immediately to thumb through your Hebrew Bible. Look up a favorite passage which you know well in

English and see if you can recognize even one Hebrew word. Your goal is a working knowledge of Biblical Hebrew, so it is wise to begin early to work with the Hebrew text. Every hour you invest will be amply repaid when you discover you can read that favorite verse with ease.

7. Finally, remember that this book, the tape, and your teacher can help, but you must do the learning. The amount of Hebrew which you will know at semester's end will be determined by how closely you follow the advice given above by two modern-day Hebrew teachers. The advice of Rabbi Hillel was given about 2000 years ago, but it too is worthy of your attention.

אל תאמר לכשאפנה אשנה שמא לא תפנה.

LISTS OF BASIC TEXTS FOR VARIOUS NEEDS

The authors of Biblical Hebrew want to emphasize that they do not intend for their text to be a complete treatment of Hebrew, only an introduction to its main elements. The following lists are provided to enable one to select sources according to one's interests and needs.

HEBREW TEXTS

Kittel's Biblia Hebraica. Third Edition. Distributed by American Bible Society (New York). Latest Printing

O. Eissfeldt, Liber Genesis, Biblia Hebraica Stuttgartensia. Distributed by American Bible Society. P.O. Box 5656, Grand Central Station, New York, N.Y. 10017

The Hebrew Bible. New York: Hebrew Publishing Co., 77-79 Delancey Street, 1914.

The Englishman's Hebrew-English Old Testament. (Genesis - II Samuel), ed. by Joseph Magil. Grand Rapids: Zondervan Publishing House, 1974.

GRAMMAR AS SUPPLEMENT TO THIS TEXT

Gesenius' Hebrew Grammar. ed. by E. Kautzsch and revised in accordance with twenty-eighth German Edition (1909) by A. E. Cowley. Oxford: at Clarendon Press, 1910.

Lambdin, T. O., Introduction to Biblical Hebrew. New York:
    Charles Scribner's Sons, 1971.

Weingreen, J., A Practical Grammar for Classical Hebrew.
    2nd Edition. Oxford: at the Clarendon Press, 1959.

LEXICAL AIDS

Brown, Francis, D.D., D.Litt., Driver, S.R., D.D., D.Litt.,
    Briggs, Charles A., D.D., D.Litt., A Hebrew & English
    Lexicon of the Old Testament. Based on Lexicon of
    William Gesenius as translated by Edward Robinson,
    Oxford: at the Clarendon Press, 1906.

Davidson, B., Analytical Hebrew and Chaldee Lexicon.
    New York: Harper & Co., n.d.

Harkavy, Alexander, Student's Hebrew and Chaldee Dictionary
    of the Old Testament. New York: Hebrew Publishing
    Co., 1914.

Koehler, Ludwig, and Baumgartner, Walter, Lexicon in Veteris
    Testamenti Libros. Grand Rapids Michigan: Wm. B. Eerd-
    man's Publishing Company, 1953.

McDaniel, Ferris L., A Reader's Hebrew English Lexicon of
    the Old Testament. Dallas, Texas: Published by author,
    1975.

Owens, John Joseph, Analytical Key to the Old Testament. Genesis,
    San Francisco: Harper & Row, Publishers, 1978.

CONTENTS

LESSON 1: LETTERS AND VOWEL POINTS

The Hebrew language in complete written form consists
in two parts, *letters* or consonants and *vowel points* or signs.
Letters are the more important part of the written language.
They convey the basic meaning(s) of words. The Vowel Points
you will learn were devised at a relatively late date as a
part of the Masoretic Text.

There are 22 (some count 23) *letters* in the Hebrew
alphabet. There are 15 *vowel points* for the various vowel
sounds. You must learn both the alphabet and the vowel points
well at the beginning of your study of Biblical Hebrew.

SCRIPT

The two scripts used in the chart below are the *square*
and the *cursive*, the former that of printed texts and the latter that of handwritten modern Hebrew. It is necessary for
you to learn and use the cursive script only if you anticipate
situations which may require use of this type script in addition to use of the square script.

THE LETTERS

Name		Square	Cursive	Final	Alternate	Translit.
אלף	Aleph	א	ﻙ			'
בית	Bet	ב	‌ב		בּ	v, b
גמל	Gimel	ג	ﻝ		גּ	g
דלת	Daleth	ד	‌ז		דּ	d
הא	He	ה	ﻥ			h

1

Name		Square	Cursive	Final	Alternate	Translit.
וו	Vav	ן	ן			v
זין	Zayn	ז	ך			z
חית	Ḥet	ח	ח			ḥ
טית	Ṭet	ט	ע			t
יוד	Yod	י	י			y
כף	Kaph	כ	⊃	ךק	כ	kh, k
למד	Lamed	ל	∫			l
מם	Mem	מ	N	ם		m
נון	Nun	נ	J	ן		n
סמך	Samekh	ס	O			s
עין	Ayin	ע	ג			ʿ
פא	Pe	פ	∂	ף	פ	f/ph, p
צדי	Ṣade	צ	∫	ץ		ṣ
קוף	Qoph	ק	ρ			q
ריש	Resh	ר	]			r
שין	Shin	שׁ	e		שׁ	š, ś
תו	Tav	ת	ʌ		ת	t

VOWEL POINTS

Name		Script	Pronunciation	
פתח	Pataḥ	ַ	a in father	אַ
קמץ*	Qameṣ*	ָ	a in father	אָ
סגול	Seghol	ֶ	e in met	אֶ
חירק	Ḥireq	ִ	i in pin	אִ

---

*This is Qameṣ Gadol (large Qameṣ). There is also Qameṣ Ḥatuph or Qameṣ Qaṭon (small Qameṣ); it occurs in a closed, unaccented syllable. It is pronounced like o in horn.

Name	Script	Pronunciation	
חירק יוד Ḥireq Yod	־ִ	i in machine	אִי
צרי Ṣere	־ֵ	e in fiance	אֵ
צרי יוד Ṣere Yod	־ֵ	e in they	אֵי
חולם Ḥolem (Dot)	־ֹ	o in mold	אֹ
חולם וו Ḥolem Vav	וֹ	o in mold	אוֹ
קבץ Qibbuṣ	־ֻ	u in bull	אֻ
שורק Shureq	וּ	u in rude	אוּ
שוא Sheva (Vocal)	־ְ	e in met	אְ
חטף פתח Ḥaṭeph Pataḥ	־ֲ	a in amount	אֲ
חטף קמץ Ḥaṭeph Qameṣ	־ֳ	o in obey	אֳ
חטף סגול Ḥaṭeph Seghol	־ֱ	e in met (short)	אֱ

PART A

Letters

𝒌 א, ALEPH, a "glottal click," is for all practical purposes not pronounced. It serves as a vowel carrier, especially at the beginning of words or syllables.

ב, BET is written and pronounced two ways: first, written at times with a dot called "daghesh lene" (d.l.), it is pronounced like b in boy; and second, without the d.l., pronounced like v in live.

ג, GIMEL, like BET is written with a d.l. at times and at

3

other times it is not. A different pronunciation was intended
for Gimel with d.l. from that of Gimel without d.l. However,
this is ignored in the pronunciation of modern Hebrew. Use
modern Hebrew for your model; pronounce GIMEL like g in go
with or without d.l.

ד,DALET, is written at times with and without d.l. Again,
although a difference in pronunciation was intended originally,
pronounce DALET like d in do with or without d.l.

Vowel Points

PATAḤ is a short horizontal line written directly under
its letter. It is pronounced like a in father. It like all
other vowels except in a special circumstance is pronounced
after the letter with which it is written.

QAMEṢ appears to be a small printed "T" under its letter.
It too is pronounced like the a in father.

SEGHOL is three dots placed in inverted triangular
fashion under a letter, pronounced like e in met.

EXERCISES

1. Following are several simple or "open" syllables
written with the letters and vowel signs which you should
now know. Note that an open syllable ends with a vowel.

ד ג ב א ד ד ד ג ג ג ב ב ב ב א א א

2. The following combinations end with a LETTER. They are "closed" syllables. Practice pronouncing them.

דַּג אָב אַב בָּא בְּא גְּא גָא בְּג בַּג דָג בַּג בְּג בַּד בָּד דָּא

VOCABULARY OF READING EXERCISE

אָב	father	גַּג	roof
אָבַד	he (it) perished	גָּד	Gad
בָּא	(he) came	דָּג	fish
בֶּגֶד	garment		

TRANSLATION EXAMPLE

גָּד אָב Gad is a father. Note that this sentence is simply two nouns juxtaposed to each other. The verb should be supplied in English. Lesson 2 contains a full explanation of sentences such as this one.

READING AND TRANSLATING

אַ בָּ גִּ דָ דָּא בְּג בָּא אָב בַּג גָּד דַּד

1. אָב, גָּד, גָּד אָב: 2. בָּא, אָב, בָּא אָב: 3. אָבַד, דָּג, אָבַד דָּג:

4. בֶּגֶד, אָבַד בֶּגֶד:

PART B

Letters

ה ,HE is pronounced like h in him.

ו ,VAV is pronounced like v in voice, same as BET without d.l. The alternative pronunciation is w in we; the name then is WAW.

5

𝟧 ז, ZAYN is pronounced like <u>z</u> in <u>z</u>ebra.

𝚷 ח, ḤET is pronounced like <u>ch</u> in a<u>ch</u> (German).

𝟨 ט, ṬET is an emphatic <u>t</u> sound pronounced for your purposes like the <u>t</u> in too.

' י, YOD is pronounced like <u>y</u> in <u>y</u>es.

Vowel Points

◌ַ ḤIREQ is one dot under a letter, pronounced like <u>i</u> in pin.

י◌ִ ḤIREQ YOD is one dot under a letter followed by a YOD; it is pronounced like <u>i</u> in machine.

◌ֵ ṢERE is two dots under a letter, pronounced like <u>e</u> in fiance.

י◌ֵ ṢERE YOD is two dots under a letter with a following YOD, pronounced like <u>ey</u> in they.

EXERCISES

Pronounce each line below until your are able to read and pronounce each syllable or word with confidence. Then copy each line on a separate sheet of paper.

1. אַ ,אָ ,אַ אִ אֵי אִ אֵ אֵי   בֵ בַ בֶ בָ בַ בֵ בֵי

2. גַ גֶ גֵ גָ גַ גֵ גִ גֵי   דַ דָ דַ דָ דִ דֵ דֵי דֵי

3. הַ הֵ הֶ הֵ הֵ הֵי הֵי   וַ וָ וֵ וֹ וִ וֵי וֵי

4. זַ זָ זֵ זִ זֵ זֵ זֵי   חַ חָ חֶ חַ חִ חֵי חֵי

5. טַ טֶ טֵ טִ טֵ טֵי טֵי   יַ יֵ יֵ יֵ יֵי יֵי

6

6. אָב, אָבָה, אָבַד, אָהַב, אָח, אֶחָד, אָחַז, אָנָה, בָּא, בֶּגֶד, פֶּתַח

7. בָּזָה, גַּד, דָּג, הָגָה, חַג, חבא. טָבַח. יָד

VOCABULARY OF READING EXERCISE

אָבָה	he was willing	הָיָה	he was
אָהַב	he loved	זָבַח	he sacrificed
אָחַז	he seized	זֶה	this (m.)
אָנָה	he desired	זָהָב	gold
אָח	brother	חַג	festival, feast
אֶחָד	one (m.)	טָבַח	he slaughtered
הָגָה	he meditated	יָד	hand

READING AND TRANSLATING

<u>Note:</u> For this and every lesson give careful attention to
the Vocabulary before attempting to read and translate an exercise.

1. אָבָה. אָבָה אָב: גַּד אָבָה: אָח אָבָה: אָהַב זָהָב: אָח אָהַב זָהָב:

2. אָב אָהַב זָהָב: אָחַז בֶּגֶד: אָח אָחַז זָהָב: אָנָה זָהָב: אָב אָנָה זָהָב:

3. אָח אָנָה בֶּגֶד: זֶה אָב: זֶה זָהָב: זָבַח. טָבַח. זָבַח אָב:

PART C

<u>Letters</u>

כ ,KAPH is another letter written at times with d.l. and
at times without it. With d.l. it is pronounced like <u>k</u> in
kite and without d.l. it is pronounced like <u>ch</u> in nach
(German). ך , final form.

7

∫ ל, LAMED is pronounced like l in look.

מ מ, MEM is pronounced like m in me. ם, ם, final form.

נ נ, NUN is pronounced like n in now. ן, ן, final form.

ס ס SAMEKH is for all practical purposes pronounced like s in sin.

ע ע, ʿAYIN is pronounced like ALEPH, or remains voiceless in Modern Hebrew. It is produced when pronounced far back in the throat. There is no English equivalent; it may be called a voiced ḤET.

Vowel Points

ֹ   HOLEM (Dot) is written usually over the upper left-hand corner of a letter. It is pronounced like o in more.

וֹ   HOLEM (Vav) is a dot over a VAV following a letter. It is pronounced like o in mold.

ֻ   QIBBUṢ is a set of three dots placed under a letter in diagonal alignment pronounced like u in bull.

וּ   SHUREQ is a VAV which contains a dot pronounced like u in rude.

PRONUNCIATION EXERCISE

(1) כֹּ, כוֹ, כֵּ, כֹה, כֵּ, כִּי, כֵּ, בַּ, פָּ, כְ   (2) לֹ, לוֹ, לָ, לֹה, לֵ, לֵ, לִי, לִי, לֵ, לַ, לֵ, לְ

(3) מֹ, מוֹ, מֶ, מוּ, מֵ, מְי, מַ, מָ, מְ   (4) נֹ, נוֹ, נֶ, נֹה, נֵ, נִי, נֵ, בְּ, נַ, בָּ, נְ

(5) סֹ, סוֹ, סֶ, סֹה, סֶ, סִי, סֶ, סַ, סְ   (6) עֹ, עוֹ, עֶ, עֹה, עֵ, עִי, עֵ, עַ, עֵ, עַ, עְ

(7) סָעַד, סָכַן, עָלַם, עוֹלָה, עֵדָה, לְבָב, חָלָה, יָדַע,[1] יָלַד, עָלָה, עָמַד

(8) חָטָא, הָיָה, יָכֹל, מָלֵא, מָלָה, נָגַד, עָמַל, עָלַז, עָטָה

VOCABULARY OF READING EXERCISE

אַיֵּה	where (is)?	עוֹמֵד	standing (m.)
אָכַל	he ate	הִנֵּה	lo, here is, behold
אֵם	mother	גַּם	also
הָלַךְ	he went, walked	עַל	on, upon
יֶלֶד	boy	הַ; הָ∙[2]	the (definite article)[2]
עָמַד	he stood	מֶה; מָה∙	what?

READING AND TRANSLATING

אַיֵּה אָב: אַיֵּה אֵם: הִנֵּה אָב: הִנֵּה אֵם: אַיֵּה הַיֶּלֶד: הַיֶּלֶד עַל

הַגָּג: גַּם אָח עַל הַגָּג: עָמַד אָח עַל הַגָּג: הַיֶּלֶד עוֹמֵד עַל הַבֶּגֶד: גַּם

עָמַד עַל־הַדָּג: הַיֶּלֶד אָחַז זָהָב: אָחַז אָח זָהָב: אָרָה אָח זָהָב: עַל

הַגָּג אָכַל אָב: אַיֵּה הַבֶּגֶד: הַבֶּגֶד עַל הַגָּג: הָלַךְ הַיֶּלֶד עַל הַגָּג:

Letters

 פ ‎פ, PE, another letter written with or without d.l., is pronounced like p in plan when d.l. is used and ph/f when d.l. is omitted. ף ‎ף , the final form.

צ ‎צ, ṢADE is another emphatic sound pronounced <u>ts</u> as in nets. ץ ‎ץ , the final form.

ק ‎ק, QOPH, also an emphatic, is pronounced like <u>q</u> in quart.

ר ‎ר, RESH is, for your purposes, satisfactorily pronounced like <u>r</u> in run.

ש ‎ש, SHIN when written with the dot over the right-hand tine is pronounced like <u>sh</u> in shin, and when written with the dot over the left-hand tine is pronounced like <u>s</u> in sin. It is then called SIN.

ת ‎ת, TAV, written with or without d.l., is to be pronounced like <u>t</u> in to for either ways of writing.

Vowel Points

SHEVA is two dots under a letter, one over the other. SIMPLE SHEVA is either SILENT or VOCAL:

SILENT SHEVA serves as a simulated vowel sign at the

end of a syllable to close that syllable and to conform to the writing principle that letters in Hebrew are nearly always written with a vowel sign in a pointed text. This SHEVA is not to be pronounced. Notice the following examples:

תִּשְׁ + מֹר = תִּשְׁמֹר . יִשְׁ + מֹר = יִשְׁמֹר . שִׁמְ + עוֹן = שִׁמְעוֹן

The SHEVA in each form analyzed closes a syllable and is silent.

VOCAL SHEVA is to be pronounced very quickly as a half or slurred vowel. A full vowel is frequently slurred or short-ened due to a shift in accent or word stress. The result is a reduction of that full vowel to SHEVA, which is expected to retain the same quality of the original vowel. However, for all practical purposes pronounce VOCAL SHEVA like e in guarded. The following hints should help you in making the distinction between a SILENT and a VOCAL SHEVA:

1. SHEVA at the beginning of a word is vocal: קְטֹל

גְּדוֹלָה , קְטַנָּה .

2. SHEVA within a word may be either silent or vocal. If it occurs with the letter that closes a syllable, it is silent. If it occurs with a letter beginning a syllable, it is vocal. In the following example, vocal and silent SHEVA occur side by side.

יִשְׁמְרוּ = יִשְׁ + מְ + רוּ
             vocal   silent

PART E

The Compound Sheva

Simple SHEVA is sometimes combined with one of three other vowels. The resulting combinations are known as the compound shevas.

HATEPH PATAH is a combination of SHEVA and the vowel Patah. Pronounce it like a in amount.

הֲ ḤAṬEPH QAMEṢ is a combination of SHEVA and the vowel Qameṣ. Pronounce it like o in obey.

הֱ ḤAṬEPH SEGHOL is a combination of SHEVA and the vowel Seghol. Pronounce it like e in met.

פֶּ, צֶ, מֶ, רֶ, שֵׁ, שֶׁ, תֵּ, בֶּ, לֵַ, סֶ, רֵַ אֶכֹל חֳלִי

VOCABULARY OF READING EXERCISE

וְ	and [וָ, בַּ, וּ]	אֶל	to (most often with verbs of motion)
נַעַר	young man	בֵּן	son
אֶרֶץ	land	אֱלֹהִים	God
עִיר	city	עָשָׂה	he made, did
שָׁמַר	he watched	לְ	to (indicates possession, precedes infinitive)
בֶּן־יַעֲקֹב	son of Jacob	בַּיִת	house
אִישׁ	man	אוֹהֵב	loves (m.)
אֵת	untranslatable particle, used to indicate a definite direct object.		

READING AND TRANSLATING

1. הָלַךְ יַעֲקֹב וְהַנַּעַר אֶל־עִיר: 2. הַנַּעַר וְהַיֶּלֶד וְהָאִישׁ עַל־הַגַּג:

3. עָשָׂה אָב אֶת־[1] הַבַּיִת: 4. בֶּן־יַעֲקֹב שָׁמַר אֶת־הַזָּהָב וְאֶת־הַבֶּגֶד:

5. מָה עָשָׂה בֶּן־יַעֲקֹב: 6. אַיֵּה יַעֲקֹב: יַעֲקֹב עַל־גַּג־הַבַּיִת:

7. אָח אוֹהֵב אֶת־הָאֱלֹהִים: 8. לָאלֹהִים[2] הָאָרֶץ[3] וְהָעִיר וְהַזָּהָב:

---

[1]Alternate spelling for אֵת. [2]לָא is an elision from לְאֱ.

[3]With the definite article, אֶרֶץ becomes הָאָרֶץ.

12

The following chart combinations are either DIPHTHONGS or CONTRACTIONS. Each combine a letter and a vowel. Study the list carefully. The transliterations are in brackets.

וַ	Diphthong:	Pataḥ and VAV	av	[av]
וָ	Diphthong:	Qameṣ and VAV	av	[av]
יַ	Diphthong:	Pataḥ and YOD	ay in aye	[ay]
יָ	Diphthong:	Qameṣ and Yod	ay in aye	[ay]
יָו	Contraction:	Qameṣ, YOD, VAV	av	[ayv]
יִו	Contraction:	Ḥireq, YOD, VAV	eve	[iv]
אָ	Contraction:	Qameṣ and Aleph	a in what	[a]
אֶ	Contraction:	Seghol and Aleph	e in they	[e]
אֵ	Contraction:	Ṣere and Aleph	e in they	[e]
הָ	Contraction:	Qames and HE	a in what	[a]
הֶ	Contraction:	Seghol and HE	e in they	[e]
הֵ	Contraction:	Ṣere and HE	e in they	[e]
יֶ	Contraction:	Seghol and YOD	e in they	[e]
יֵ	Contraction:	Ṣere and YOD	e in they	[e]

גָּלֶה סוּסֶיךָ סוּסֶיבֻה סוּסַי סוּסֵי סוּסָיו אָבְיוּ קָרָא יִמְצָא יִמָּצֵא

גָּלָה יִגְּלֶה

NOUNS		VERBS		PARTICLES	
אֵם	אָב	טָבַח	אָבַד	זֶה	אֶל
יֶלֶד	בֶּגֶד	שָׁמַר	בָּא	אַיֵּה	לְ
נַעַר	גַּג	אָכַל	אָבָה	הִנֵּה	אֵת
בֵּן	גַּד	הָלַךְ	אָהַב	גַּם	
בֶּן־יַעקב	אָח	עָמַד	אָחַז	עַל	
אֶרֶץ	אֶחָד	עָשָׂה	אָרָה	הַ־	
אֱלֹהִים	זָהָב	עוֹמֵד	הָגָה	מַה־	
בַּיִת	חָג	אוֹהֵב	הָיָה	וְ	
אִישׁ	יָד		זָבַח		
	עִיר				

EXCURSUS, IMPORTANT LETTERS, TERMS, AND MARKS

BEGED KEPHET

You have already seen that the letters ב ג ד כ פ ת, the so-called "beged-kephet" letters, occur at times with an inner marking and at other times without that marking or dot. The dot within these six letters may be either "daghesh lene" or "daghesh forte". The sentence or word situation will be the clue for determining whether the dot is d.l. or d.f. Read the following explanations concerning the use and purpose intended for these dots.

BEGED KEPHET AND DAGHESH LENE

The daghesh lene was intended to indicate a "stop" or "explosive" sound under certain circumstances. Looking at the following examples, you will notice that d.l. stands in a beged-kephet letter whenever that letter begins a word or a syllable. More importantly, the letter is not preceded immediately by a vowel!

בֶּגֶד גָּלָה דָּבָר כָּתַב פָּעַל תָּמֵהּ יִכְתּוֹב צְפַרְדֵּעַ

By the omission of d.l., the punctuators of the text intended to indicate a "continuous" or a "spirantized" type of pronunciation for a beged-kephet letter. Observe:

אָב בֶּגֶד אָכַל בְּרַךְ אָסַף יוֹסֵף הֵלֵךְ כָּרַת דָּבָר

In the light of the examples given above, two observations may be made.

1. The d.l. is omitted when a vowel occurs immediately preceding the beged-kephet letter. The "continuous" aspect of the vowel sound is understood to influence the pronunciation of the consonant to change from a "stop" to a "spirant". Thus with the omission of d.l., the punctuators intended to show a continuous pronunciation for the beged-kephet letter.

2. The pronunciation you are learning is used by a majority of Hebrew professors and by Israelis speaking in modern Hebrew. Note that you are using two different sounds for BET, KAPH, and PE but only one for GIMEL, DALET, and TAV.

DAGHESH FORTE

Daghesh Forte (דגש חזק, i.e., "strong dot") is a dot within a letter intended to indicate the doubling of that letter. That is, the Masoretes used d.f. to indicate in writing a double pronunciation, rather than writing the letter itself twice. For example, they chose to write אַיֵּה, "where?" instead of אַיְיֵה.

In the Masoretic Text (MT), the d.f. is used in a variety of word, phrase, and sentence situations. Some of the more common usages are indicated below.

1. Doubling or strengthening a letter. The most frequent occurrence of d.f. is with any letter except the laryngaels and RESH (see below) in order to indicate that double pronunciation is necessary. Examples:

a. a part of the orthography of particles: מַה־זֶּה, הַבֵּן.

b. a part of the orthography of nouns: גִּבּוֹר, צִפּוֹר.

c. a part of the orthography of verbs: דִּבֵּר, מְדַבֵּר.

2. Doubling resulting from assimilation. Daghesh forte is used to indicate a doubling resulting from the assimilation of one consonant to another. Assimilation is a frequent phonetic change which you will encounter often as you progress to reading the Hebrew Bible. Take note of this use of d.f. and refer back to this explanation when necessary.

מִזֶּה < "from this" מִן זֶה

Explanation: The d.f. in זּ is intended to show that זּ must be given a double pronunciation because the ן of מִן has assimilated to it.

3. Doubling the beged-kephet letters. The dot for d.f. is exactly the same as the dot for d.l. in the beged-kephet letters. Whenever d.f. occurs with a beged-kephet letter, it indicates not only the "stop" pronunciation but also a double pronunciation.

הַבֵּן hab-ben, "the son"

גִּבּוֹר gib-bor, "warrior"

THE LARYNGAELS

The laryngaels are א ,ה ,ח ,ע. Each one represents a sound for which there is no exact equivalent in English. These four letters, along with ר, share several characteristics which will become increasingly evident as you proceed with your study of Hebrew. Read the comments below and then observe the examples which are given. You will no doubt refer back to this list many times throughout the semester.

1. The laryngaels and RESH are not easily doubled in spoken Hebrew; they are purposely not doubled in writing. Herein is the reason for stating that the d.f. may occur in any letter except a laryngael or RESH. When one would expect doubling, but the presence of a laryngael or RESH prevents that doubling, the preceding vowel is often lengthened for compensation.

a. Not הַאָב but הָאָב "the father".

b. Not הַעִיר but הָעִיר "the city".

c. Not הַרוּחַ but הָרוּחַ "the wind".

2. Laryngaels and RESH prefer a-class vowels. Because the laryngaels and RESH linguistically have an inherent a-vocalic aspect, you will notice that they are nearly always pointed with a-class vowels. This causes variations in the normal vocalization patterns of both nouns and verbs.

3. Laryngaels prefer compound SHEVA. This phenomenon too will be illustrated in later lessons.

4. A laryngael at the end of a word frequently takes a gliding or helping Patah. This help is used only with a final ח or ע and is the only Hebrew vowel to be pronounced before its consonant within a syllable.

רוּחַ rû-aḥ, "wind"   זְרוֹעַ z^e-rô-a^c, "arm"

STRESS

Stress is a word used synonymously with accent. In Hebrew, the stress normally falls on the last syllable of a word: קָטַל דָּבָר. The main exception to this rule is the Segholate noun, or the noun whose last vowel is (or at one time was) a Seghol: מֶלֶךְ, יֶלֶד, etc.

THE MAIN MARKS OF PUNCTUATION

1. סוֹף פָּסוּק(:) SOPH PASUQ is two dots at the end of a verse in the Hebrew Bible.

2. סִלּוּק(ּ) SILLUQ designates the accented syllable of the last word in a verse. It is a vertical mark beside the vowel point of the syllable in which it occurs. That syllable is thus "in pause". That is, the speaker ought to pause longer in pronouncing it that he usually does, because the end of the verse is approaching. The "pausal" form of a word regularly exhibits a lengthened vowel with SILLUQ.

3. אתנח(ּ) ATHNAH is a small, wishbone-shaped sign which occurs to mark the end of the first half of a verse. It marks the accented syllable of the word which signals the end of that half. Words marked with the אתנח are also placed in pause.

17

Here is an illustration of the three marks which are listed above, using Genesis 1:1:

בְּרֵאשִׁית בָּרָא אֱלֹהִים אֵת הַשָּׁמַיִם וְאֵת הָאָרֶץ׃

OTHER FREQUENTLY-USED MARKS

1. מקף. Maqqeph, "binder", is a short horizontal line which connects two, three, or four words. The combined words are then treated as one for purposes of accent.

עַל־הַגָּג   אֶת־כָּל־אֲשֶׁר־לוֹ

2. מתג. Metheq, "bridle", is a short line written with an open syllable at the beginning of a word (in appearance, exactly like Silluq!). Metheq indicates that one is to read with care the unusual syllable which it marks. For example, Metheq may note the persistence of a long vowel which, two syllables removed from the accent, would normally reduce to Sheva: אָנֹכִי. It may also mark a short vowel in a pre-stress position which normally requires a closed syllable: תַעֲמֹד. But by far the most frequent usage of Metheq occurs when a reader is being warned that a following Sheva is <u>vocal</u>:

קָרְאָה אָכְלָה קוֹרְאָה שָׁמְעוּ

3. מפיק. Mappiq is a dot written in a final ה to indicate that it is a full consonant.

סוּסָה גְּמַלָּהּ[1]

SPECIAL NOTE

There are many other marks which occur in the twenty-one non-poetic books of the Hebrew Bible. A complete list may be found in <u>Gesenius' Hebrew Grammar</u>.[2]

---

[1]מפיק can also occur with the letters י, ו, א, but this usage is not followed by most printed editions of the Bible.

[2]Pages 56-67 of the 28th edition.

LESSON 2: THE NOUN SENTENCE

NOUN SENTENCE DEFINED

The noun sentence is the simplest form of a sentence in Hebrew. It is a sentence whose subject is a noun and whose predicate is another noun or an adjective. It may be composed of two nouns or of one noun and one adjective. In either case, the one is juxtaposed to the other. The proper form of the copula (verb "to be" in English) is understood in Hebrew but supplied in the English translation. The tense of the verb is determined from context. Lacking proper contextual clues, the present tense is to be assumed. Study the following examples carefully.

אַבְרָהָם אִישׁ׃   Abraham is a man.

אַבְרָהָם זָקֵן׃   Abraham is old.

The normal order of the noun sentence is subject-predicate. This order may be inverted for emphasis:

אִישׁ אַבְרָהָם׃   Abraham is [only] a man.

LEARNING VOCABULARY

טוֹב	good	קָדוֹשׁ	holy
יוֹסֵף	Joseph	גָּדוֹל	large
זָקֵן	old	אַבְרָהָם	Abraham
יִצְחָק	Isaac	קָטָן	small
דָּן	Dan		

19

READING AND TRANSLATING

1. ‏אַבְרָהָם אִישׁ:‏

2. ‏יוֹסֵף אִישׁ:‏

3. ‏גָּד אִישׁ:‏

4. ‏יִצְחָק אִישׁ:‏

5. ‏דָּן אִישׁ:‏

6. ‏אַבְרָהָם אָב:‏

7. ‏אַבְרָהָם אָח:‏

8. ‏אַבְרָהָם זָקֵן:‏

9. ‏אַבְרָהָם גָּדוֹל:‏

10. ‏אַבְרָהָם קָדוֹשׁ:‏

11. ‏אִישׁ יוֹסֵף:‏

12. ‏אָח יִצְחָק:‏

13. ‏דָּן בֵּן:‏

14. ‏אָב אַבְרָהָם:‏

15. ‏בֵּן גָּד:‏

16. ‏יוֹסֵף טוֹב:‏

17. ‏גָּד קָטָן:‏

18. ‏אַבְרָהָם קָדוֹשׁ:‏

19. ‏עִיר גְּדוֹלָה:‏

20. ‏יִצְחָק זָקֵן:‏

LESSON 3: THE VERB: QAL PERFECT

THE QAL PERFECT--STRONG VERB

The verb in Hebrew is the most important part of speech; the noun is next in importance. The Hebrew verb consists in a number of different stems which are variations of a three-lettered or triliteral verbal root. Further, the verb in Hebrew is characterized by well-developed inflectional endings which convey the grammatical concepts person, number, and gender.

"Qal Perfect" may be understood as terminology that applies to forms intended to express past, active action. Here is the Qal Perfect with the root שמר.

שָׁמַ֫רְתִּי	I watched	שָׁמַ֫רְנוּ	we watched
שָׁמַ֫רְתָּ	you (m.) watched	שְׁמַרְתֶּם	you (m.) watched
שָׁמַ֫רְתְּ	you (f.) watched	שְׁמַרְתֶּן	you (f.) watched
שָׁמַ֫ר	he watched	שָׁמְר֫וּ	they (c.) watched
שָׁמְרָה	she watched		

Descriptive Linguistic Analysis

1. On a separate sheet of paper, list the inflectional endings of the Qal Perfect and state the function of each ending.

2. What might be called the characteristic vowel pattern for the Qal Perfect?

GRAMMATICAL TERMS

1. MOOD. Mood, sometimes called mode, applies to
the attitude or set of mind of the personal subject of the
verb. Mood is ascertained mainly from context; there is
not a particular aspect of the inflectional ending which
indicates mood. Indicative mood is understood for the Qal
stem in Hebrew, for it is the stem of straightforward de-
clarative force. In Hebrew, the general vocalization pattern of the Qal is perhaps the main clue to the indicative
mood.

2. VOICE. The term voice applies to the relation
of the action to the speaker. This also is an aspect of a
verb that is subsumed under or included in the force of the
Qal stem. In the Qal Perfect, active voice is indicated or
understood. That is, the speaker or doer says or does the
action suggested by the verb. This naturally applies only
to transitive verbs and not to stative or voluntary verbs.

3. TENSE. The term tense applies to time-point.
This is also an aspect of the verb which is understood by
the general pattern of vocalization of the Qal Perfect.
More specifically, Qal Perfect is understood to indicate
completed action or past tense. Note that "past tense" is
not an exact English equivalent to "Qal Perfect" in Hebrew.
English past tense is, however, a close equivalent to Hebrew
perfect tense.

4. PERSON. The term person applies to the speaker
or doer situation. Qal Perfect inflectional endings vary
in order to show the person who is speaking or acting.

5. GENDER. The term gender applies to male or female distinctions. Hebrew has only male and female gender,
lacking a neuter gender designation. The inflectional endings of the Qal Perfect also indicate this gender distinction.
Note that the term gender is a linguistic classification but
is not equal to sexual classification. The word אֹזֶן is a
feminine noun whether one is speaking of a man's ear or a
woman's ear.

6. NUMBER. Number is a term which applies to those
endings which indicate either singular or plural. Hebrew
does use a "dual" number, but it is limited to a few nouns
which will be studied later.

VOCABULARY OF EXERCISE

אָכַל he ate   אָמַר he said

הָלַךְ he walked, went   יָשַׁב he dwelt, sat

נָתַן he gave   אָהַב he loved

קָרָא he called, read   עָמַד he stood

שָׁמַע he heard   מִי who?

בְּ in   בָּ , בַּ in the

אֶל to   קוֹל voice, sound

מָקוֹם place   דָּבָר word, thing

לֶחֶם bread, food   סֵפֶר book

READING AND TRANSLATING

1. שָׁמַעְתִּי אֶת־הַדָּבָר׃

2. אָכַלְתִּי לֶחֶם בָּעִיר׃

3. אָמַרְתִּי דָבָר אֶל־אָב׃

4. הָלַכְתִּי אֶל־יְרוּשָׁלַיִם׃

5. הָלַכְתִּי אֶל בֵּית־לָחֶם׃

6. יָשַׁבְתָּ בָּעִיר הַזְּקֵנָה׃[1]

7. קָרָאתָ אֶל־אַבְרָהָם׃

8. עָמַדְתָּ בַּמָּקוֹם הַטּוֹב׃

9. עָמַדְתָּ בַּמָּקוֹם הַגָּדוֹל׃

10. שָׁמַעְתָּ אֶת־הָאִישׁ הַזָּקֵן׃

11. אָכַלְתָּ אֶת הַלֶּחֶם הַקָּטָן׃

12. אָמַרְתָּ אֶת־הַדָּבָר הַטּוֹב׃

13. אָכַל אַבְרָהָם אֶת הַלֶּחֶם׃

14. אָמַר דָּן אֶת־הַדָּבָר׃

15. הַבֵּן אָהַב אֶת־יִצְחָק׃

16. יָשְׁבָה רָחֵל בְּבֵית לָחֶם׃

17. קָרְאָה אֶל הָאִישׁ הַזָּקֵן׃

18. שָׁמְעָה אֶת־הַדָּבָר׃

19. הָלְכָה לֵאָה אֶל־יְרוּשָׁלַיִם׃

20. שָׁמַע אֶת־הַדָּבָר הַטּוֹב׃

21. שָׁמַרְנוּ דָבָר טוֹב׃

22. הָלַכְנוּ אֶל־הָעִיר׃

23. שְׁמַעְתֶּם אֶת־קוֹל אַבְרָהָם׃

24. אֲכַלְתֶּם אֶת־הַלֶּחֶם הַטּוֹב׃

25. הֲלַכְתֶּן אֶל־הַמָּקוֹם הַקָּדוֹשׁ׃

26. קְרָאתֶן בְּקוֹל גָּדוֹל אֶל־אַבְרָהָם׃

27. אָכְלוּ לֶחֶם זָקֵן בְּעִיר זְקֵנָה׃

28. נָתְנוּ לֶחֶם וְסֵפֶר לְיִצְחָק׃

---

[1] This is the feminine form of the adjective זקן.

23

LESSON 4: THE NOUN: MONOSYLLABIC NOUNS

THE MORPHOLOGY OF THE NOUN

Many Hebrew nouns are derivatives of triliteral roots and are usually bi-syllabic formations. They will be introduced later. Other nouns are derivatives of bi-literal roots or derive from modification of a triliteral root. A noun of this type is monosyllabic.

All Hebrew nouns are understood to have gender significance grammatically, including nouns which designate inanimate objects. There is no neutral or neuter gender in Hebrew, only masculine and feminine.

Hebrew nouns are formed with particular endings or a lack of ending to indicate number, state, and gender.

There are three number endings: singular, plural, and dual (used only with certain words or situations).

"State" will be explained in a later lesson.

THE MONOSYLLABIC NOUN FORMATION

	M		F	
Sg.	סוּס	horse	סוּסָה	mare
Pl.	סוּסִים	horses	סוּסוֹת	mares

By looking at the endings listed above, you should be able to add correct endings to the following words:

פר bull   פר cow

פר bulls   פר cows

Only a few nouns will employ this full set of gender endings. Normally, whether masculine or feminine, a noun employs only the endings for its grammatical and/or sexual gender.

COMMON IRREGULAR NOUNS

A number of very common nouns are exceptions to the general pattern of nominal inflection given above. Study carefully the words below, for they occur frequently in the Hebrew Bible.

אָב	father	אָבוֹת	fathers
אֵם	mother	אִמּוֹת	mothers
בֵּן	son	בָּנִים	sons
בַּת	daughter	בָּנוֹת	daughters
אִישׁ	man	אֲנָשִׁים	men
אִשָּׁה	woman	נָשִׁים	women

REVIEW AND DRILL

On a separate sheet of paper, write the Qal Perfect of שמר and ישב.

VOCABULARY OF EXERCISE

אָב, אָבוֹת	father		סוּס, סוּסִים	horse
אֵם, אִמּוֹת	mother		פַּר, פָּרִים	bull
בֵּן, בָּנִים	son		סֵפֶר	book
בַּת, בָּנוֹת	daughter		זָקֵן	old
אִישׁ, אֲנָשִׁים	men		נָתַן	he gave
אִשָּׁה, נָשִׁים	women			

READING AND TRANSLATING

1. שָׁמַרְתִּי פַּר וְסוּס:

2. הָלַכְתָּ עַל הַסּוּס אֶל־יְרוּשָׁלַיִם:

3. נָתַן סֵפֶר וְדָג טוֹב:

4. שָׁמְרוּ אֶת הַפָּרָה וְאֶת־הַסּוּסָה:

5. אֲמַרְתֶּם דָּבָר טוֹב אֶל־הָאִשָּׁה:

6. קָרְאוּ אֶת־הַסֵּפֶר:

7. שָׁמְרוּ פָּרִים וְסוּסִים:

8. אֲהַבְתֶּן אָבוֹת וְאִמּוֹת וּבָנוֹת וּבָנִים:

9. הֲלַכְתֶּם עַל הַסּוּסִים אֶל יְרוּשָׁלַיִם:

10. דָּן נָתַן פָּרִים וּפָרוֹת לְאַבְרָהָם:

11. אָמְרוּ דָּבָר טוֹב אֶל הַנָּשִׁים:

12. לֵאָה נָתְנָה לָהֶם לַאֲנָשִׁים:[1]

13. אֲנָשִׁים וְנָשִׁים קָרְאוּ בַסֵּפֶר:

14. אַבְרָהָם נָתַן סוּסִים לָאִישׁ הַזָּקֵן:

---

[1] לָהֶ = לָהֵ.

READING GENESIS 22:1-2

Beginning here, each lesson will conclude with a reading passage from Genesis which you will not be expected to understand when you first see and hear it. There are several simple steps which you should take in studying all biblical passages. First, listen to the passage on the tape. Second, try to read the passage aloud on your own. Third, listen to the tape again, repeating each phrase in the pause provided. Fourth, listen to and reread on your own the entire passage. Fifth, use the helps given in the textbook to translate and understand what you have heard and read.

ויהי   "and it was." The root is היה, "he/it was."

אחר   "after" (adverb).

אלה   "these" (demonstrative pronoun, plural).

נסה   "(He) tested." Root: נסה.

ויאמר   "And he said." Past tense of אמר.

קח נא   "Take now." קח is the imperative form of לָקַח, "he took." נא is an emphatic particle, "please."

בנך   "your son." בן plus a pronominal suffix ך.

יחידך   "only one." Note the pronominal suffix which is added to the form יחיך.

אשר   "whom."

לך לך   "go, you yourself." Root: הלך

מריה   "Moriah."

עלה   "he went up, ascended."

העלה   "to offer up." This is a "causative form" based on the root letters עלה.

העלהו   "offer him up." עלה is the root of העלהו.

עֹלָה   "a burnt offering." This is a noun which literally means "something that ascends."

הר   "mountain." Plural: הָרִים.

אֹמַר   "I shall say/tell." In this verse, "I shall point out/designate."

אֵלֶיךָ   "to you." Preposition אל with a suffix.

שָׁם   "there."

SPECIAL NOTE

In this and all subsequent passages from the Hebrew Bible, the notes are given with unpointed Hebrew words only, unless a special form demands extra attention. In this way, you will become acquainted with Hebrew as it was first written and as it is once being written in Modern Israel.

LESSON 5: THE NOUN: SEGHOLATES, PRONOMINAL SUFFIXES

THE SEGHOLATE NOUN

The "Segholate" nouns are one of several classes of bi-syllabic nouns in Hebrew. They may be called a special class because of two features which characterize them only: (1) The second vowel is SEGHOL in most cases except in a word with medial or final LARYNGAEL; (2) the stress is on the first syllable of the singular form.

COMMON SEGHOLATE NOUNS

מֶלֶךְ	king	מְלָכִים	kings
יֶלֶד	boy	יְלָדִים	boys
בֶּגֶד	garment	בְּגָדִים	garments
אֶרֶץ	land, country	אֲרָצוֹת	lands, countries
לֶחֶם	bread	no plural form	
רֶגֶל	foot	רַגְלַיִם	feet
בֹּקֶר	morning	בְּקָרִים	mornings
אֹזֶן	ear	אָזְנַיִם	ears
נַעַר	lad, young man	נְעָרִים	lads, young men
בַּעַל	Baal, owner, lord	בְּעָלִים	Baals, owners, lords
סֵפֶר	book	סְפָרִים	books

29

OBSERVATIONS ON SEGHOLATE NOUNS

1. There are three classes of segholate nouns. Each noun is classified according to the vowel which it had in the original form from which its biblical form is derived. The three classes are:

a-class מֶלֶךְ   i-class סֵפֶר   u-class בֹּקֶר

2. The segholates are nearly always masculine. Only רֶגֶל ,אֶרֶץ, and אֹזֶן in the list above are feminine.

3. Whether masculine or feminine in gender, a segholate noun prefers the following vowel pattern in the plural: ים ָ ְ .

4. אָזְנַיִם is really a "dual" form, to be studied in lesson 6.

5. A few segholates have Paṭaḥ as a vowel in the singular because of a medial laryngael. The laryngael is usually ע as in בַּעַל or נַעַר above.

6. The plural of a segholate noun beginning with a laryngael shows compound rather than simple sheva. Example: אֲבָנִים, "stones."

PRONOMINAL SUFFIXES WITH ל

לִי	to me	לָנוּ	to us
לְךָ	to you (m.)	לָכֶם	to you (m.)
לָךְ	to you (f.)	לָכֶן	to you (f.)
לוֹ	to him/it	לָהֶם	to them (m.)
לָהּ	to her/it	לָהֶן	to them (f.)

OBSERVATIONS ON PRONOMINAL SUFFIXES

1. Hebrew employs suffixes to convey both the dative ("to" or "for") and the accusative (direct object) idea.

2. The pattern of ל plus pronominal suffixes pre-
vails also with other one-consonant prepositions like ב or
כ. For "in them," an alternate form (בָּם) is often used in
place of בָּהֶם.

3. The suffixes are also used as possessive indi-
cators with nouns, objective particles with verbs, and a
variety of other things. You will learn more about Hebrew
suffixes in later lessons.

READING AND TRANSLATING

1. הָלַךְ עַל הַסּוּס אֶל יְרוּשָׁלַיִם׃

2. נָתְנוּ לוֹ אֶת הַדָּג וְאֶת־הַסֵּפֶר׃

3. שָׁמְרוּ אֶת־הַפָּרִים וְהַסּוּסִים לָהֶם׃

4. הָלְכוּ עַל סוּסִים אֶל־בֵּית־לֶחֶם׃

5. רִבְקָה אָהֲבָה אֶת־יִצְחָק וְיוֹסֵף אָהַב אֶת־רָחֵל׃

6. נָתְנָה לִי לֵאָה לֶחֶם׃

7. נָשִׁים וַאֲנָשִׁים קָרְאוּ לָכֶם ‎*מִן־הַסֵּפֶר׃   "from"*

8. אַבְרָהָם נָתַן סוּסִים לָאִישׁ הַזָּקֵן׃

9. הוּא נָתַן לָהּ סוּס׃   (הוּא is the pronoun "he")

10. לָנוּ נָתַן הָאֱלֹהִים אֶת־הָאָרֶץ׃

READING GENESIS 22:3-4

Read verse three and four aloud from your Hebrew
Bible. Then listen to the tape and read them again. Now
study the vocabulary given below and try to understand as
much of the passage as you can.

וישכם   "and he arose early." The root is השכים.

ויחבש   "and he bound." Root _____?

חמר   "donkey." חמרו   "his donkey."

31

וַיִּקַּח‎ "and he took." Root: לָקַח‎.

שְׁנֵי‎ "two of."

נְעָרָיו‎ "his young men." Root _____?

אִתּוֹ‎ "with him."

וַיְבַקַּע‎ "and he cut/divided." Root: בָּקַע‎.

עֲצֵי‎ "the wood for."

וַיָּקָם‎ "and he got up." Root: קוּם‎.

וַיֵּלֶךְ‎ "and went." Root: הָלַךְ‎.

מָקוֹם‎ "place."

בַּיּוֹם‎ "on the day."

הַשְּׁלִישִׁי‎ "the third." Note that the adjective follows its
     noun. Translate: "on the third day."

וַיִּשָּׂא‎ "and he lifted up." Root: נָשָׂא‎.

עֵינָיו‎ "his eyes." Singular: עַיִן‎.

וַיַּרְא‎ "and he saw." Root: רָאָה‎.

מֵרָחֹק‎ "from a distance." מֵ‎ is the shortened form of מִן‎.

32

Vocabulary Review Lessons 1 - 5

These words should be learned before going on to Lesson 6.

סוּסִים	טוֹב	הָלַךְ	אָב
סוּסוֹת	יוֹסֵף	יָלַד	אָבַד
פַּר	זָקֵן	עָמַד	בָּא
פָּרָה	יִצְחָק	עוֹמֵד	בֶּגֶד
פָּרִים	דָּן	הִנֵּה	גָּג
פָּרוֹת	קָדוֹשׁ	גַּם	גָּד
בַּת	גָּדוֹל	עַל	דָּג
אִשָּׁה	אַבְרָהָם	הֵ, הַ	אָבָה
אָבוֹת	קָטֹן	הֶ, הַ; הֶ	אָהַב
אִמּוֹת	נָתַן	מַה; מָה	אָחַז
בָּנִים	קָרָא	וְ (וָ, וִ, וּ)	אוֹרָה
בָּנוֹת	שָׁמַע	נַעַר	אָח
אֲנָשִׁים	כִּי	אֶרֶץ	אֶחָד
נָשִׁים	מָקוֹם	עִיר	הָגָה
מֶלֶךְ	לֶחֶם	שָׁמַר	הָיָה
רֶגֶל	אָמַר	בֶּן־יַעֲקֹב	זֶבַח
בָּקָר	יָשַׁב	אִישׁ	זֶה
אֹזֶן	מִי	אֵת	זָהָב
פֹּעַל	כַּ; כָּ	אֶל	חַג
	קוֹל	בֵּן	טֶבַח
	דָּבָר	אֱלֹהִים	יָד
	סֵפֶר	עָשָׂה	אַיֵּה
	סוּס	לְ	אָכַל
	סוּסָה	בַּיִת	אִם
		אוֹהֵב	

LETTERS AND VOWEL POINTS

It is <u>very important</u> to learn the Letters, Vowel Signs, and Diphthongs and Contractions before proceeding to the next lesson. The charts below are started as suggestion for you to use on a work sheet until you have completely mastered each chart with its several items.

THE LETTERS

Name	Script Cursive	Final Form	Translit.	Pronunciation
Bet	בּ בּ		b	'b' in boy
etc.				

THE VOWEL POINTS

Name	Script	Transliteration	Pronunciation
Pataḥ	בַ	a	'a' in father
etc.			

DIPHTHONGS AND CONTRACTIONS

Name	Script	Pronunciation	Trans'n
Diph., Pataḥ and VAV	וַ	av	(av)
etc.			

LESSON 6: THE DUAL, THE CONJUNCTION

THE DUAL AS NUMBER IN BIBLICAL HEBREW

At an early period in the history of the Hebrew language, the "dual" was used as extensively in classical texts as it is in Arabic. However, it has been retained in those biblical texts at our disposal only in limited usage. Many of the functions of the dual have been taken over by plural forms in biblical Hebrew.

Hebrew uses a dual ending to indicate the number two with nouns which name parts of the body that come in pairs (as well as a limited number of other words). The ending characteristic of the "dual" is -aym. Below is a list of the most common nouns which retain a dual form.

יָד	hand	יָדַיִם	two hands	יָדוֹת	hands
רֶגֶל	foot	רַגְלַיִם	two feet	רְגָלִים	feet/times
אֹזֶן	ear	אָזְנַיִם	two ears		
עַיִן	eye	עֵינַיִם	two eyes	[עֲיָנוֹת]	eyes
כָּנָף	wing	כְּנָפַיִם	two wings	[כְּנָפוֹת]	wings
קֶרֶן	horn	קַרְנַיִם	two horns	קְרָנוֹת	horns
פַּעַם	time	פַּעֲמַיִם	two times, twice	פְּעָמִים	times

Note that all the words listed above are feminine!

Several nouns which occur frequently in classical Hebrew retain a dual ending in spelling but not in function or meaning. That is, the dual ending signifies merely the nominal ending, not the idea of two-ness, duality, or numerality in any way.

מַיִם water   מִצְרַיִם Egypt

שָׁמַיִם heaven(s)   יְרוּשָׁלַיִם Jerusalem

LEARNING VOCABULARY

Learn all of the nouns listed in this lesson. Then review the vocabulary lists given in previous lessons before attempting the exercises which are written below.

THE SPELLING OF ו

The conjunction "and" (ו) immediately precedes the word with which it occurs; it is an "inseparable particle." As the principle co-ordinating conjunction of Hebrew, it is used to connect words, phrases, and clauses. The VAV is normally pointed with SIMPLE SHEVA (וְ), but it may also be spelled in other ways.

1. ו is written וּ in two situations:

a. preceding a word that begins with a labial:

דָּוִד וּבִנְיָמִין   David and Benjamin

אֲחַשְׁוֵרוֹשׁ וְרַשְׁתִּי   Ahasuerus and Vashti

לֶחֶם וּמַיִם   bread and water

סוּסִים וּפָרוֹת   horses and cows

b. preceding a word with an initial SHEVA and any first letter except YOD:

גְּדוֹלָה וּקְטַנָּה   large and small

2. ו may precede a word with an initial Ḥataph.
When it does, it is **vocalized** with the full vowel component
of the following Ḥataph:

וַאֲנִי   and I;   וֶאֱדֹם   and Edom;   וָאֳנִיָּה   and a ship

3. Preceding an initial YOD with VOCAL SHEVA, the
ו becomes part of a contraction:

וִירוּשָׁלַיְם   and Jerusalem;   וִיהוּדָה   and Judah

4. Preceding a word which stresses the syllable
that immediately follows it, ו is frequently vocalized with
QAMEṢ. This spelling applies mainly to words which end a
sentence or a clause:

טוֹב וָרָע   good and evil

דָּת וָדִין   law and judgment

5. Preceding the special form יֹּאמֶר, ו is vocalized
with Pataḥ:

וַיֹּאמֶר [וְיֹאמֶר]   and/then he said

6. Preceding the special form אֹמַר, ו is vocalized
with Qameṣ:

וָאֹמַר   and/then I said

ו WITH DIVINE NAMES

1. Because the Tetragrammaton exhibits special
features, there are special problems attached to the way
in which ו is vocalized preceding it. The four letters
יהוה should be pronounced as if they were the four letters
אדני. Accordingly, a preceding ו should be vocalized with
Pataḥ (see rule 2 above): וַיהוה, "and Yahweh," should be
pronounced וַאדֹנָי.

2. The word אלהים exhibits special features also
when it is preceded by ו. One would expect וֶאֱלֹהִים in the
light of rule 2 above. However, the Hebrew Bible very con-
sistently spells וֵאלֹהִים.

37

READING AND TRANSLATING

1. הַיֶּלֶד וְהַנַּעַר לָקְחוּ* אֶת־הַסֵּפֶר: took*

2. הִנֵּה הַבַּעַל בָּעִיר הַזְּקֵנָה:

3. לָאִישׁ עַיִן וְרֶגֶל וְאֹזֶן וְיָד:

4. לָאִישׁ יָדַיִם וְאָזְנַיִם וְרַגְלַיִם וְעֵינָיִם:

5. לְנָשִׁים יָדוֹת וְרַגְלַיִם וַאֲזָנַיִם בַּעֵינוֹת:

6. אָהֵב יְלָדִים וּנְעָרִים אֶת־הָאֱלֹהִים:

7. לְפַּר קָרְנַיִם וּלְצִפּוֹר (bird) כְּנָפַיִם:

8. הָלַךְ אָב אֶל־אֶרֶץ מִצְרַיִם פַּעֲמָיִם:

9. עָשָׂה אֱלֹהִים אֶת־הַשָּׁמַיִם וְאֵת הָאָרֶץ:

READING GENESIS 22:5-6

שְׁבוּ לָכֶם   "you (boys) stay here." שְׁבוּ is an imperative form from the root יָשַׁב.

פֹּה   "here."

עִם   "with."

נֵלְכָה   "we will go." Root: הָלַךְ.

עַד כֹּה   "as far as over there." A difficult phrase to translate exactly.

וְנִשְׁתַּחֲוֶה   "and we will worship." The root, which is either הוה or שׁחה, means either to worship or to cast oneself down prostrate to the ground in humility.

וְנָשׁוּבָה   "and we will return." Root: שׁוּב.

אֲלֵיכֶם   "to you." with a suffix.

38

וישם   "and he put." Root: שִׂים.

בידו   "in his hand." This is a threefold combination:
        בְּ plus יָד plus the suffix וֹ.

אש   "fire."

מאכלת   "knife."

וילכו   "and they went." Root: הלך.

שניהם   "the two of them."

יחדו   "together."

REVIEW OF THE NOUN

This chart should be mastered before going on to Lesson 7.

Masc. Sing.	Masc. Plural	Fem. Sing.	Fem. Plural
Monosyllabic Nouns			
סוּס	סוּסִים	סוּסָה	סוּסוֹת
פָּר	פָּרִים	פָּרָה	פָּרוֹת
Bisyllabic Nouns			
נָבִיא	נְבִיאִים	נְבִיאָה	נְבִיאוֹת
אָסִיר	אֲסִירִים	אֲסִירָה	אֲסִרוֹת
בְּכוֹר	בְּכוֹרִים	בְּכוֹרָה	בְּכֹרוֹת
Segholate Nouns			
יֶלֶד	יְלָדִים	יַלְדָּה	יְלָדוֹת
מֶלֶךְ	מְלָכִים	מַלְכָּה	מְלָכוֹת
נַעַר	נְעָרִים	נַעֲרָה	נְעָרוֹת
בֹּקֶר	בְּקָרִים	✕	✕

Dual Forms	Singular	Dual	Plural
	יָד	יָדַיִם	יָדוֹת
	יוֹם	יוֹמַיִם	יָמִים
	רֶגֶל	רַגְלַיִם	רְגָלִים

40

LESSON 7: THE ADJECTIVE

Like the noun, the adjective endings in Hebrew are used to indicate gender (masculine or feminine) and number (singular or plural). In the following chart, notice that the adjectival endings are identical with those of the noun which you have learned earlier.

	Singular	Plural
Masculine	#	־ים
Singular	־ָה	־וֹת

ATTRIBUTIVE USAGE

The attributive adjective follows the noun which it modifies. It also agrees with that noun in number, gender, and determination (i.e., it takes the article if its noun has the article). Note the following examples:

בֵּן גָּדוֹל	a big son
הַבֵּן הַגָּדוֹל	the big son
בַּת גְּדוֹלָה	a big daughter
הַבַּת הַגְּדוֹלָה	the big daughter
בָּנִים גְּדוֹלִים	big sons
הַבָּנִים הַגְּדוֹלִים	the big sons
בָּנוֹת גְּדוֹלוֹת	big daughters
הַבָּנוֹת הַגְּדוֹלוֹת	the big daughters

41

PREDICATIVE USAGE

The adjective as predicate agrees with its antecedent noun or pronoun in gender and number, but not in determination. That is, it does not take the definite article.

גְּדוֹל הַבֵּן (or) הַבֵּן גָּדוֹל	The son is big.
הַבַּת גְּדוֹלָה	The daughter is big.
הַבָּנִים גְּדוֹלִים	The sons are big.
הַבָּנוֹת גְּדוֹלוֹת	The daughters are big.

Note that the statement בן גדול is ambiguous. The context must determine whether it means "a son is big" or simple "a big son."

SUBSTANTIVE USAGE

The Hebrew adjective may be used as a "substantive" (noun) as in the case of many other languages [Cf. Greek ho kalos, "the good man"].

אברהם הזקן בעיר:	Abraham is the old man in the city.
יהודה החכם בבית־לחם:	Judah is the wise man in Bethlehem.

FORMATIONS OF MONOSYLLABIC AND BISYLLABIC ADJECTIVES

Hebrew grammar does not make a distinction between a noun and an adjective. You will notice later in the complete discussions of the noun that the formations are precisely the same as those to be presented in this lesson for the Hebrew adjective. There are extensive numbers of these adjectival/nominal formations. Below are the basic or more frequent formations for monosyllabic and bisyllabic words.

A. Monosyllabic adjectives may be classified under three similar categories:

a.   An unchangeable long vowel which stays the same regardless of the endings which are added:

$$\text{good} \quad \text{טוֹב} \quad \text{טוֹבָה} \quad \text{טוֹבִים} \quad \text{טוֹבוֹת}$$

$$\text{empty} \quad \text{רֵיק} \quad \text{רֵיקָה} \quad \text{רֵיקִים} \quad \text{רֵיקוֹת}$$

b.   A short vowel which is lengthened when, because endings are added, it occurs in a pre-stressed position:

$$\text{evil} \quad \text{רַע} \quad \text{רָעָה} \quad \text{רָעִים} \quad \text{רָעוֹת}$$

c.   A short vowel which remains, plus a doubled second consonant. These words are derivatives of roots which exhibit the same letter in both the second and third position:

$$\text{strong} \quad \text{עַז} \quad \text{עַזָּה} \quad \text{עַזִּים} \quad \text{עַזּוֹת}$$

$$\begin{matrix}\text{numerous,} \\ \text{much, many}\end{matrix} \quad \text{רַב} \quad \text{רַבָּה} \quad \text{רַבִּים} \quad \text{רַבּוֹת}$$

B. Bisyllabic adjectives exhibit two main formations which are illustrated below.

a.   Adjectives which begin with a letter other than one of the laryngaels. These words (1) reduce an initial Qameṣ to Sheva, (2) retain the long vowel in the second syllable, and (3) add proper endings. The following common adjectives are good examples of this class:

$$\text{גָּדוֹל} \quad \text{קָרוֹב} \quad \text{קָדוֹשׁ} \quad \text{יָשָׁר} \quad \text{תָּמִים}$$

b.   Adjectives which begin with a laryngael. These words (1) reduce an initial Qameṣ to a compound Sheva, (2) keep the second vowel, and (3) add the proper ending. Examples of this class include:

$$\text{חָזָק} \quad \text{חָכָם} \quad \text{עָשִׁיר}$$

VOCABULARY OF EXERCISE

שֶׂה   lamb   עָרַךְ   he put in rows, arranged

43

בָּנָה	he built		עָקַד	he bound
מִזְבֵּחַ*	altar		רֵיק	empty, vain
רַע	evil, bad		חָזָק	strong
תָּם	complete, perfect		רָחוֹק	far, distant
קָרוֹב	near, close		יָשָׁר	upright, righteous
תָּמִים	whole, complete		עַז	strong
עָשִׁיר	rich		רַב	numerous, much, many

*Pataḥ pronounced after ח; it is Pataḥ Furtive.

EXERCISES

1. Translate the masculine singular form of these monosyllabic adjectives and complete the forms required to make them feminine singular and then plural:

רֵיק   עַז   רַע

2. Do the same thing for these bisyllabics without initial laryngael:

זָקֵן   גָּדוֹל   יָשָׁר

3. Now the same thing for these bisyllabics with initial laryngael:

חָזָק   חָכָם   עָשִׁיר

READING AND TRANSLATING

1.   הַיֶּלֶד הַגָּדוֹל חָזָק׃

2.   הַנַּעֲרָה הַקְּטַנָּה טוֹבָה׃

44

3. הָאֲנָשִׁים הַזְּקֵנִים עֲשִׁירִים:

4. הַנְּעָרִים הָעַזִּים רָעִים:

5. הַמָּקוֹם הַקָּדוֹשׁ קָרוֹב:

6. הָעִיר הַגְּדוֹלָה רְחוֹקָה:

7. יוֹסֵף וְרָחֵל יָשְׁבוּ בְּבֵית־לֶחֶם הָעִיר הַזְּקֵנָה:

8. קְרָאתֶן אֶת־הַדְּבָרִים הַטּוֹבִים לְדָן:

9. הַנְּעָרִים הָלְכוּ אֶל־יְרוּשָׁלַיִם עַל־הַסּוּסִים הַגְּדוֹלִים:

10. הָאִישׁ הֶחָכָם אָמַר דְּבָרִים רַבִּים וְטוֹבִים בָּעִיר:

READING GENESIS 22:7-9

ויבאו   "and they came." Root: בּוֹא.

יראה   "He [God] will see." Root: רָאָה. The familiar way of translating this phrase by "God will provide" does not reflect the context accurately. Abraham would have killed his son because he could not <u>see</u> the animal which God had specially provided in <u>a</u> bush behind him. But God could and did <u>see</u> how to solve Abraham's problem. The writer of the story is very clever in using ראה in this way.

ויבן   "and he built." Root: _____ ?

הנני   "here I am." הנה with a suffix.

ויערך   "and he arranged." Root: _____ ?

ויעקד   "and he bound." Root: _____ ?

ממעל   "on top of."

אתו   "him." Here used as the direct object of וישם.

REVIEW OF THE ADJECTIVE

This chart should be mastered before going on to Lesson 8.

Monosyllabic adjectives: (a), (b), and (c) indicate examples of categories mentioned on page 43.

Masc. sing.	Fem. Sing.	Masc. Plural	Fem. Plural
(a) טוֹב	טוֹבָה	טוֹבִים	טוֹבוֹת
(c) עַז	עַזָּה	עַזִּים	עַזּוֹת
(c) רַב	רַבָּה	רַבִּים	רַבּוֹת

Bisyllabic Adjectives

Masc. sing.	Fem. Sing.	Masc. Plural	Fem. Plural
(a) גָּדוֹל	גְּדוֹלָה	גְּדוֹלִים	גְּדוֹלוֹת
(b) יָשָׁר	יְשָׁרָה	יְשָׁרִים	יְשָׁרוֹת

	(With initial laryngael)		
(a) חָכָם	חֲכָמָה	חֲכָמִים	חֲכָמוֹת
(b) עָשִׁיר	עֲשִׁירָה	עֲשִׁירִים	עֲשִׁירוֹת

Bisyllabic Adjectives: Miscellaneous types.

Masc. sing.	Fem. Sing.	Masc. Plural	Fem. Plural
יָפֶה	יָפָה	יָפִים	יָפוֹת
קָשֶׁה	קָשָׁה	קָשִׁים	קָשׁוֹת

LESSON 8: THE INSEPARABLE PREPOSITIONS

Certain Hebrew prepositions are called "inseparable" because they attach directly to the word before which they are used, and thus appear to be prefixes. The inseparable prepositions are:

בְּ in, with, by;   לְ to, for;   כְּ as, like.

These inseparable prepositions may be compared with the separable or independent prepositions:

אֶל to(ward);   מִן from;   עַד unto;   עִם with

בֵּין between;   עַל on, upon, about, concerning, near

There are also many compound prepositions which will be studied later.

VOCALIZATION OF INSEPARABLE PREPOSITIONS

Before considering the vocalization of the inseparable prepositions, reread and carefully review the different ways in which וְ is vocalized (pp. 36-37).

Now examine the charts below, noticing the pointing of בְ, לְ, and כְ in comparison with that of וְ.

וֵאלֹהִים and God   לֵאלֹהִים to God

כֵּאלֹהִים in God   כֵּאלֹהִים like God

47

וְסֵפֶר	and a book	לְסֵפֶר	to a book
בְּסֵפֶר	in a book	כְּסֵפֶר	like a book
וִיהוּדָה	and Judah	לִיהוּדָה	to Judah
בִּיהוּדָה	in Judah	כִּיהוּדָה	like Judah
וַאֲרִי	and a lion	לַאֲרִי	to a lion
בַּאֲרִי	in a lion	כַּאֲרִי	like a lion
וֶאֱדֹם	and Edom	לֶאֱדֹם	to Edom
בֶּאֱדֹם	in Edom	כֶּאֱדֹם	like Edom
וָאֲנִיָּה	and a ship	לָאֲנִיָּה	to a ship
בָּאֲנִיָּה	in a ship	כָּאֲנִיָּה	like a ship

INSEPARABLE PREPOSITIONS BEFORE VOCAL SHEVA

Two vocal shevas at the beginning of a word or phrase were not pronounced one after the other by the Masoretes. Except for words that begin with י (see above), the following rules apply when an inseparable preposition is attached to a word with an initial vocal Sheva: (a) the vocal Sheva of the word becomes silent; and (b) the Sheva of the inseparable preposition becomes Hireq. Note the following examples:

לִשְׁלֹמֹה to Solomon; בִּשְׁלֹמֹה in Solomon;

כִּשְׁלֹמֹה like Solomon.

Remember that ו before a word with initial vocal Sheva (except initial יְ) becomes וּ: וּשְׁלֹמֹה and Solomon.

48

INSEPARABLE PREPOSITIONS WITH DETERMINED NOUNS

When the inseparable preposition occurs with a definite noun (i.e., a noun with the article ה prefixed to it), the letter ה of the article is dropped and the vowel of the article becomes the vowel of the preposition:

לֶהָרִים	to the mountains	BECOMES	לְהָרִים
לַמֶּלֶךְ	to the king	BECOMES	לְהַמֶּלֶךְ
לָאָרֶץ	to the land	BECOMES	לְהָאָרֶץ
לָעִיר	to the city	BECOMES	לְהָעִיר

ETC.

LEARNING VOCABULARY

שָׁלַח	to send forth	מַלְאַךְ	messenger, angel
הִנֵּה	here is, behold	עַתָּה	now
אֱנוֹשׁ	man, mankind	סְבַךְ	thicket
שָׁמַיִם	heavens	מַאֲכֶלֶת	knife
שָׁחַט	to slaughter, slay	אַיִל	ram, hart
אֲרִי	lion	אַיֵּה	where?
מַלְכָּה	queen	גָּמָל	camel

READING AND TRANSLATING

1. ‏אָמַר דְּבָרִים טוֹבִים לְאִישׁ זָקֵן:‏
2. ‏הָלְכָה עַל־חֲמוֹר בְּעִיר קְטַנָּה:‏

49

3. הַיְלָדִים הָלְכוּ כַּמֶּלֶךְ:

4. נָתְנוּ סְפָרִים לַמְּלָכִים זְקֵנִים:

5. הָלְכָה בִּבְגָדִים קְטַנִּים אֶל־יְרוּשָׁלַיִם:

6. הַיְלָדִים קָרְאוּ סְפָרִים כִּנְעָרִים טוֹבִים:

7. הַחֲמוֹרִים אָכְלוּ כִּגְמַלִּים:

8. נָתַן שְׁלֹמֹה הַזָּקֵן אֶת־הַלֶּחֶם לִיהוּדָה:

9. נָתַן אַבְרָהָם אֶת־הַסּוּסִים לִיהוּדָה:

10. נָתְנָה הַמַּלְכָּה אֶת־הַבְּגָדִים לִירוּשָׁלַיִם:

11. יִצְחָק וְלֵאָה הָלְכוּ אֶל־עִיר קְטַנָּה בְּאָדָם:

12. הַיֶּלֶד קָרָא כַּאֲרִי לִיהוּדָה:

13. אֱלֹהִים אָמַר דְּבָרִים רַבִּים לָאֱנוֹשׁ:

14. בַּבַּיִת יָשְׁבוּ הַיְלָדִים:

15. כַּמַּלְכָּה אָהַב הַמֶּלֶךְ לֶחֶם:

16. לַסּוּס רַגְלַיִם גְּדוֹלוֹת:

READING GENESIS 22:10-12

וישלח   "and he sent forth," i.e., stretched out in preparation for action. Root: שלח.

לשחט   "to slay." This is an infinitive form of שחט.

ויקרא   "then, he called."

אל   a common negative particle.

תשלח   "[do not] send forth." תשלח is here used as an imperative form of שלח.

אל תעש   "do not do." תעש is here used as an imperative form of עשה.

מאומה   "anything."

50

ידעתי   "I know." Root: ידע.

ירא   "a fearer of ..." Cf. יָרֵא, to fear, be afraid.

אתה   "you." This is the second person masculine singular form of the independent personal pronoun which will be fully explained in the next lesson.

לא   "not." This is another common negative particle.

חשכת   "you have [not] withheld." Root: חשך.

יחיד   "unique, only, single."

ממני   "from me." This is a combination of מן plus a suffix. See lesson 9 for complete explanations of the separable prepositions with pronominal suffixes.

LESSON 9: INDEPENDENT PERSONAL PRONOUNS

THE INDEPENDENT PERSONAL PRONOUNS

The independent personal pronouns in Hebrew are used
only in nominative contexts -- as subjects, or agreeing in
form with subjects of a sentence. They are not used as the
direct objects of a verb or as objects of a preposition.

Singular		Plural	
אֲנִי, אָנֹכִי	I	אֲנַ֫חְנוּ, נַ֫חְנוּ, אֲנַ֫ה	we
אַתָּה	you (m)	אַתֶּם	you (m)
אַתְּ	you (f)	אַתֵּ֫ן, אַתֵּ֫נָה	you (f)
הוּא	he/it	הֵם, הֵ֫מָּה	they (m)
הִיא	she/it	הֵ֫נָּה, הֵן	they (f)

Notice that some of these pronouns developed variant
form(s) due to frequent usage in everyday speech. Note also
that some pronouns, particularly second person forms, seem
to be associated with the inflectional endings of the verb.

You must learn the independent personal pronouns
well, for they occur in virtually every passage which you
will ever read from the Hebrew Bible.

1. הוּא לָקַח אֶת־הַסְּפָרִים:

2. הִיא לָקְחָה אֶת־הַסְּפָרִים:

3. אֲנִי לָקַחְתִּי אֶת־הַסְּפָרִים:

4. וַאֲנַחְנוּ לָקַחְנוּ אֶת־הַסְּפָרִים:

5. הֵם לָקְחוּ אֶת־הַסְּפָרִים:

6. אַתֶּם לְקַחְתֶּם אֶת־הַזָּהָב:

7. הָאִישׁ מִן הָעִיר הָלַךְ:

8. הִנֵּה הָלְכוּ מִבֵּית לָחֶם:

9. וַאֲנַחְנוּ הָלַכְנוּ מִירוּשָׁלַיִם:

10. הִיא הָלְכָה מֵחֶבְרוֹן:

11. אֲנִי קָרָאתִי וְהַסּוּס קָרֵב:

12. אַתְּ קָרָאת וְהַסּוּסָה קָרְבָה:

13. וַאֲנַחְנוּ קָרָאנוּ וְהַסּוּסִים קָרְבוּ:

14. הַסְּפָרִים הַגְּדוֹלִים נָפְלוּ עֲלֵיהֶם:

READING GENESIS 22:13-15

וַיִּשָּׂא   "and he lifted up." Root: נשא.

וַיַּרְא   "and he saw." Root: ראה.

אַחַר   "after." Here, implying "back of" or "behind."

נֶאֱחַז   "caught." A passive [Niphal] form of אחז, to seize, grasp.

בקרניו   "by its horns." Dual noun, קֶרֶן, with a suffix.

וילך   "and he went." Root: הלך.

יעלהו   "he offered it." Root עלה with a suffix.

תחת   "in place of." Literally, "under."

ויקרא   "and [Abraham] called." Root: קרא.

שם   "the name of."

ההוא   "that." In this position, the pronoun functions as a demonstrative.

יהוה יראה   "YHWH will see to/take care of." This is the same verb, ראה, used in earlier verses so cleverly.

אשר   "because."

יאמר   "it was said." A passive [Niphal] form of אמר.

היום   "today."

יראה   "it [i.e., this matter of a sacrifice] has been seen to."

שנית   "a second [time]."

שמים   "heaven."

Vocabulary Review Lessons 6 - 9

These words should be learned before going on to Lesson 10.

יָד	עַז	הוּא
עַיִן	רַב	הִיא
כָּנָף	פִּי	אֲנַחְנוּ, נַחְנוּ, אֲנוּ
קֶרֶן	מִן	אַתֶּם
פַּעַם	עַד	אַתֵּן, אַתֵּנָה
מַיִט	עֵט	הֵם, הֵמָּה
שָׁמַיִם	בֵּין	הֵנָּה, הֵן
מִצְרַיִם	הַר	נָשָׂא
יְרוּשָׁלַיִם	שָׁלַח	רָאָה
אֱדֹם	אֱנוֹשׁ	אַחַר
יְהוּדָה	שָׁחַט	אָחַז
שֶׂה	אֲרִי	עָלָה
עֶרֶךְ	מַלְקָה	תַּחַת
בָּנָה	מַלְאָךְ	שָׁם
מִזְבֵּחַ	עַתָּה	יהוה
רַע	סָבַךְ	אֲשֶׁר
תָּם	מַאֲכֶלֶת	אָמַר
קָרוֹב	אַיִן	יוֹם
תָּמִים	גָּמָל	שֵׁנִי
עָפִיר	נָפַל	
עָקַד	קְרָב	
רִיק	אֲנִי, אָנֹכִי	
חָזָק	אַתָּה	
יָשָׁר	אַתְּ	

INSEPARABLE PREPOSITIONS WITH

PRONOMINAL SUFFIXES

Notice those suffixes with singular nouns are those with the inseparable prepositions and the particle

SINGULAR	בְּ	לְ	אֵת	Pattern
1st common	בִּי	לִי	אֹתִי	ִי
2nd masculine	בְּךָ	לְךָ	אֹתְךָ	ךָ ְ
2nd feminine	בָּךְ	לָךְ	אֹתָךְ	ךְ ָ
3rd masculine	בּוֹ	לוֹ	אֹתוֹ	וֹ
3rd feminine	בָּהּ	לָהּ	אֹתָהּ	הּ ָ
PLURAL				
1st common	בָּנוּ	לָנוּ	אֹתָנוּ	נוּ ָ
2nd masculine	בָּכֶם	לָכֶם	אֶתְכֶם	כֶם ְ
2nd feminine	בָּכֶן	לָכֶן	אֶתְכֶן	כֶן ְ
3rd masculine	*בָּהֶם	לָהֶם	אֹתָם	ם ָ
3rd feminine	בָּהֶן	לָהֶן	אֹתָן	ן ָ

* בָּם is also used.

The pronominal suffix in Hebrew performs a number of grammatical functions, as you have already seen. In this lesson, special attention is given to pronominal suffixes used with singular nouns, a usage roughly equivalent to the possessive pronoun(s) in English. Study the forms of the chart below, pronounce them aloud several times, and make your own translation of them.

SUFFIX	MASCULINE NOUNS			FEMININE NOUNS		
Sg 1c <u>my</u> יִ	סוּסִי	מַלְכִּי	דְּבָרִי	סוּסָתִי	אֹשְׁתִּי	תוֹרָתִי
2m <u>your</u> ךָ	סוּסְךָ	מַלְכְּךָ	דְּבָרְךָ	סוּסָתְךָ	אֹשְׁתְּךָ	תוֹרָתְךָ
2f <u>your</u> ךְ	סוּסֵךְ	מַלְכֵּךְ	דְּבָרֵךְ	סוּסָתֵךְ		תוֹרָתֵךְ
3m <u>his</u> וֹ	סוּסוֹ	מַלְכּוֹ	דְּבָרוֹ	סוּסָתוֹ	אֹשְׁתוֹ	תוֹרָתוֹ
3f <u>her</u> הָ	סוּסָהּ	מַלְכָּהּ	דְּבָרָהּ	סוּסָתָהּ		תוֹרָתָהּ
Pl 1c <u>our</u> נוּ	סוּסֵנוּ	מַלְכֵּנוּ	דְּבָרֵנוּ	סוּסָתֵנוּ		תוֹרָתֵנוּ
2m <u>your</u> כֶם	סוּסְכֶם	מַלְכְּכֶם	דְּבַרְכֶם	סוּסַתְכֶם		תוֹרַתְכֶם
2f <u>your</u> כֶן	סוּסְכֶן	מַלְכְּכֶן	דְּבַרְכֶן	סוּסַתְכֶן		תוֹרַתְכֶן
3m <u>their</u> ם	סוּסָם	מַלְכָּם	דְּבָרָם	סוּסָתָם		תוֹרָתָם
3f <u>their</u> ן	סוּסָן	מַלְכָּן	דְּבָרָן	סוּסָתָן		תוֹרָתָן

SPECIAL NOTES

1.   Suffix endings and connecting vowels remain constant with most nouns, mono- or bi-syllabic.

2.   The vocalization of nouns with more than two syllables requires several different patterns to be introduced later.

READING AND TRANSLATING

1. הָלַכְתִּי אֶל־הָעִיר עַל־סוּסִי:

2. שָׁמַעְתִּי אֶת־אִשְׁתִּי:

3. שָׁמַעְתָּ אֶת־מַלְכְּךָ:

4. עַל־סוּסְךָ הָלַכְתָּ אֶל־הָעִיר:

5. שָׁמְעָה אֶת־דְּבָרֵךְ:

6. הָלַכְתְּ אֶל־הָעִיר עַל־סוּסֵךְ:

7. הוּא קָרָא אֶת־תּוֹרָתוֹ:

8. הוּא הָלַךְ אֶל־הָעִיר עַל־סוּסוֹ:

9. הִיא שָׁמְעָה אֶת־דְּבָרוֹ:

10. הִיא הָלְכָה אֶל־הָעִיר עַל־סוּסָם:

11. רָאִינוּ*אֶת־מַלְכֵּנוּ:

12. אֲנַחְנוּ הָלַכְנוּ עַל־סוּסָתְכֶם:

13. אַתֶּם שְׁמַעְתֶּם אֶת־סוּסְכֶם:

14. אַתֶּן הֲלַכְתֶּן עַל־סוּסְכֶן:

15. אַתֶּן שְׁמַעְתֶּן אֶת־תּוֹרַתְכֶן:

16. אַתְּ הָלַכְתְּ עַל־סוּסֵךְ:

*from רָאָה, "to see".

58

בי ‏ "to Myself." "by Myself."

נשבעתי ‏ "I have sworn." Root: שבע.

נאם יהוה ‏ "utterance of the LORD." May be rendered "says Yahweh."

כי יען ‏ "because." Two separate particles which mean different things when used individually.

עשית ‏ "you have done." Root: עשה.

ברך אברכך ‏ "I will really bless you."

הרבה ארבה ‏ "I will greatly multiply [your seed]."

כוכבי ‏ "the stars of." Cf. כּוֹכָב, a star.

חול ‏ "sand."

שפת הים ‏ "beach." Lit., "lip [i.e., edge] of the sea."

ירש ‏ "[your seed] will inherit/possess." Root: ירש.

שער ‏ "gate/entrance."

איביו ‏ "his enemies." Cf. אֹיֵב, enemy, foe.

התברכו ‏ "[they] will be blessed." Root: ברך.

בזרעך ‏ "by [through] your seed."

כל ‏ "all."

גויי ‏ "the nations of."

הארץ ‏ "the world."

עקב אשר ‏ "because."

וישב ‏ "then [Abraham] returned." Root: שׁוּב.

ויקמו ‏ "and they arose." Root: קוּם.

וישב ‏ "So [Abraham] lived." Root: ישב.

LESSON 11: PRONOMINAL SUFFIXES WITH PLURAL NOUNS

Consonantally, the pronominal suffixes used with plural nouns are essentially the same as those used with singular nouns studied in Lesson 10. Study the chart below, noting carefully the major difference -- a longer connecting vowel.

SUFFIXES		MASCULINE		FEMININE
Sg 1c	ַי	סוּסַי	מְלָכַי	סוּסוֹתַי
2m	ֶיךָ	סוּסֶיךָ	מְלָכֶיךָ	סוּסוֹתֶיךָ
2f	ַיִךְ	סוּסַיִךְ	מְלָכַיִךְ	סוּסוֹתַיִךְ
3m	ָיו	סוּסָיו	מְלָכָיו	סוּסוֹתָיו
3f	ֶיהָ	סוּסֶיהָ	מְלָכֶיהָ	סוּסוֹתֶיהָ
Pl 1c	ֵינוּ	סוּסֵינוּ	מְלָכֵינוּ	סוּסוֹתֵינוּ
2m	ֵיכֶם	סוּסֵיכֶם	מְלָכֵיכֶם	סוּסוֹתֵיכֶם
2f	ֵיכֶן	סוּסֵיכֶן	מְלָכֵיכֶן	סוּסוֹתֵיכֶן
3m	ֵיהֶם	סוּסֵיהֶם	מְלָכֵיהֶם	סוּסוֹתֵיהֶם
3f	ֵיהֶן	סוּסֵיהֶן	מְלָכֵיהֶן	סוּסוֹתֵיהֶן

SEPARABLE PREPOSITIONS WITH

PRONOMINAL SUFFIXES

Notice that the suffixes of plural nouns are used with the separable pronouns in most instances. Refer again to p. 60.

Singular	אֶל	עַל	עַד	עִם	מִן	Pattern
1st common	אֵלַי	עָלַי	עָדַי	עִמִּי*	מִמֶּנִּי	יָ
2nd masculine	אֵלֶיךָ	עָלֶיךָ	עָדֶיךָ	עִמְּךָ	מִמְּךָ	יךָ
2nd feminine	אֵלַיִךְ	עָלַיִךְ	עָדַיִךְ	עִמָּךְ	מִמֵּךְ	יךְ
3rd masculine	אֵלָיו	עָלָיו	עָדָיו	עִמּוֹ	מִמֶּנּוּ	יו
3rd feminine	אֵלֶיהָ	עָלֶיהָ	עָדֶיהָ	עִמָּהּ	מִמֶּנָּה	יהָ

PLURAL						
1st common	אֵלֵינוּ	עָלֵינוּ	עָדֵינוּ	עִמָּנוּ	מִמֶּנּוּ	ינוּ
2nd masculine	אֲלֵיכֶם	עֲלֵיכֶם	עֲדֵיכֶם	עִמָּכֶם	מִכֶּם	יכֶם
2nd feminine	אֲלֵיכֶן	עֲלֵיכֶן	עֲדֵיכֶן	עִמָּכֶן	מִכֶּן	כֶן
3rd masculine	אֲלֵיהֶם	עֲלֵיהֶם	עֲדֵיהֶם	עִמָּם**	מֵהֶם	יהֶם
3rd feminine	אֲלֵיהֶן	עֲלֵיהֶן	עֲדֵיהֶן	עִמָּן	מֵהֶן	יהֶן

* עִמָּדִי is also used.

** עִמָּהֶם is also used.

READING GENESIS 22:20-24

ויהי "and it was." Root: היה.

אחרי "after."

[ו]יגד "it was made known." A Passive [Hophal] form of the root נגד.

לאמר "saying." In form, this is an infinitive. Its function is to introduce a direct quotation. The ל, "to," serves as the determinative [marker for] of the Hebrew infinitive construct to be studied later. The root of לאמר is אמר.

הוא "she." This is an alternate spelling of the third person feminine singular independent personal pronoun found only in the Pentateuch.

אחיך "your brother." אח, "brother," adds suffixes to its singular form with the connecting י normally used only in plural nouns. Cf. אָחִיו, "his brother," in vs. 21 below. Another very common noun which does the same thing when adding suffixes to its singular form is אב. "Your father" is אָבִיךָ. Note that the form אֲחִי means "the brother of;" and אֲבִי means "the father of."

בכור "first-born [son]."

ילד "to beget, bear."

פילגש "concubine."

ותלד "And she gave birth." Root: ילד.

62

LESSON 12: THE PRONOUN: INTERROGATIVE AND DEMONSTRATIVE

THE INTERROGATIVE PRONOUN

You have already learned and used some of the Hebrew interrogative pronouns. Those which you have seen in a previous lesson and some new ones are listed below. Note the way in which each pronoun may function.

1. מִי and its various uses.

a. מִי "who?" is used most frequently to ask or introduce a question.

מִי הָאִישׁ: Who is the man?

מִי הָלַךְ אֶל־בֵּית־לֶחֶם: Who went to Bethlehem?

b. מִי "whose?" When used in this way, מִי is usually governed by a special type of noun ["construct"] which will be introduced in a later lesson.

בַּת־מִי־אָתְּ: Whose daughter are you?

c. מִי "whom?" When used with the sign of the definite direct object, מִי is translated by the English objective case.

בַּחֲרוּ ... אֶת־מִי תַּעֲבֹדוּן: Choose ... <u>whom</u> you will serve.

Note that מִי is also translated "whom" when it is the object of the prepositions בְּ, לְ, אֶל, עִם, etc.

2. מָה/מַה "what?" is used mainly to refer to things. Variations in spelling occur on account of an initial laryngael in the word which immediately follows it or because of

an accent shift.

מַה תִּתֶּן לִי: What will you give to me? (Gn. 15:2)

מַה שְׁמֶךָ:   What is your name?

מָה אַתָּה רֹאֶה: What do you see? (Jer. 1:11)

מֶה עָשִׂיתָ:   What have you done?

3. אֵי and אַיֵּה "where?" The former is used mainly with suffixes, the latter with complementary nouns.

אַיֶּכָּה   Where are you? (Gn. 3:9)

אַיֵּה שָׂרָה אִשְׁתֶּךָ:   Where is Sarah your wife? (Gn. 18:9)

4. לָמָה "Why?" למה means either "why" or "for what purpose/reason?"

לָמָה חָרָה לָךְ:   Why are you angry?

לָמָה תַעֲמֹד בַּחוּץ: Why do you stand outside?

5. כַּמָּה/כַּמֶּה "How much/how many?" Each spelling expresses both how much and how many. Both spellings are a combination of כ and מה.

כַּמָּה יְמֵי שְׁנֵי חַיֶּיךָ:   How many are the days of the years of your life? (Gn. 47:8)

כַּמָּה רָחְבָּהּ וְכַמָּה אָרְכָּהּ:   How much is its width and how much is its length? (Zech. 2:6)

6. "When?" מָתַי is a specific word in Hebrew that means "when." It usually refers to a future time. To express the temporal idea of when, Hebrew uses a different construction altogether, one which will be introduced later.

THE DEMONSTRATIVES

You have already seen the demonstratives "this" and "these," which may be used as pronouns or as adjectives. In Hebrew, the words "that" and "those" are expressed by using the independent personal pronouns in a special position as illustrated below.

64

	THIS	THAT	THESE	THOSE
Masculine:	זֶה	הוּא	אֵ֫לֶּה	הֵם
Feminine:	זֹאת	הִיא	אֵ֫לֶּה	הֵן

The demonstratives, like adjectives, may be used in the predicate or the subject position. Note carefully the examples given below:

זֶה הָאִישׁ	This is the man.
אֵ֫לֶּה הַנָּשִׁים	These are the women.
זֹאת הַיַּלְדָּה	This is the girl.

Here are some examples of the demonstrative in its attributive usage:

הָאִישׁ הַזֶּה	this man
הָאִשָּׁה הַזֹּאת	this woman
הָאֲנָשִׁים הָאֵ֫לֶּה	these men
הַנָּשִׁים הָאֵ֫לֶּה	these women
הָאִישׁ הַהוּא	that man
הָאִשָּׁה הַהִיא	that woman
הָאֲנָשִׁים הָהֵם	those men
הַנָּשִׁים הָהֵן	those women

READING GENESIS 23:1-4

וַיִּהְיוּ חַיֵּי שָׂרָה	"Now the life of Sarah was ..."
מֵאָה	"one hundred."
עֶשְׂרִים	"twenty."
שָׁנָה	"years." This is a singular form which is conventionally used with numbers higher than ten.

שבע   "seven." Note the plural of שָׁנָה, שָׁנִים.

ותמת   "then she died." Root: מות.

קרית ארבע   "Kiryat-Arba." Place name.

ויבא   "So [Abraham] went." Root: בוא.

לספד   "to lament, mourn." This is an infinitive form of ספד.

לבכתה   "to weep for her." Infinitive form of בכה.

ויקם   "then he arose." Root: קום.

פני   "the presence of."

מתו   "his dead [one]."

גר   "stranger, sojourner."

תושב   "sojourner."

תנו   "Give!" A Qal imperative form of נתן.

אחזת קבר   "a burial site." Lit., a possession of a grave.

ואקברה   "so that I may bury." Root: קבר.

מלפני   "out of my sight, from my presence."

LESSON 13: THE RELATIVE PRONOUN

AN INDECLINABLE PRONOUN OF RELATION

The pronoun אֲשֶׁר may be translated who, which, whom, or that, depending upon circumstances of context. It is a "sign of relation," because it serves as a connecting link between a main clause and a subordinate one. Thus it must often be supplemented by a pronominal suffix or a word like שָׁם at the end of the subordinate clause in order to define the intended relationship more precisely. Following are some examples which illustrate the functions of אֲשֶׁר.

1. אֲשֶׁר without a supplement is used as a simple relative pronoun:

עַל אַחַד הֶהָרִים אֲשֶׁר אֹמַר אֵלֶיךָ   "... upon one of the mountains which I will say [i.e., point out] to you."

קַח־נָא אֶת־בִּנְךָ ... אֲשֶׁר אָהַבְתָּ   "Take now your son ... whom you love."

2. אֲשֶׁר is often supplemented by an adverb or by a pronominal suffix at the end of a subordinate clause:

אֶל הָאָרֶץ אֲשֶׁר יָצָאתָ מִשָּׁם   "to the land from which you came."

מִבְּנוֹת הַכְּנַעֲנִי אֲשֶׁר אָנֹכִי יוֹשֵׁב בְּקִרְבּוֹ

"from the daughters of the Canaanites among whom I live"

בקרבו, "in their midst," is the supplement required because אֲשֶׁר merely connects the second half of the sentence with the antecedent הכנעני.

3. אשר is also combined with other particles [בַּאֲשֶׁר, מֵאֲשֶׁר, כַּאֲשֶׁר]. Such combinations should be learned in context.

READING GENESIS 23:5-10

ויענו   "Then [the Hittites] answered." Root: ענה.

שמעונו   "Listen to us." This is a plural imperative of שמע with the first person plural suffix.

נשיא   "prince of." Lexical form: נָשִׂיא.

בתוכנו   "in our midst." Cf. תוך, "midst, middle."

במבחר   "in the best of." מבחר is a selection, choice, or, as here, "the select," i.e., "the best."

קברינו   "our graves." Cf. קֶבֶר, a grave.

קבר   "bury!" Imperative form.

לא יכלה ממך   "[he] will not prevent you."

מקבר   "from burying." This entire phrase, איש ממנו את קברו לא יכלה ממך מקבר מתך, may be translated: "no one among us will withhold from you his burial site [as a place for] burying your dead [wife]."

וישתחו   "and he prostrated himself."

וידבר   "Then he spoke." A Piel [intensive] form of the root דבר.

אתם   "with them."

אם   "if."

יש נפשכם   "such is your desire." יֵשׁ means "there is" or "there are." נֶפֶשׁ is the life [principle].

שמעוני   "Listen to me."

פגעו   "bring near."

בעפרון   "Ephron." Here the ב points to the direct object of the verb.

ויתן   "that he may give." Root: נתן.

מערת   "the cave of." Lexical form: מְעָרָה.

בקצה   "in the corner of." Lexical form: קָצֶה.

שדהו   "his field." שָׂדֶה, "field," plus an alternate form of the third masculine singular suffix, הו.

בכסף   "for money."

מלא   "full." The phrase בכסף מלא means "for a fair price."

יתננה   "let him give it [the cave]." Root: נתן.

ויען   "and he answered." Root: ענה.

באזני   "in the ears of."

שער   "a gate." לכל באי לשער עירו means "to all who come to the gate of the city."

SPECIAL NOTE

The phrase עם הארץ in verse seven simply means "the people of the land/country." In later, rabbinic Hebrew, it was this phrase that acquired the meaning of people who are untutored or ignorant, i.e., the masses, with whom should be contrasted the well-trained [in the Torah] Rabbis.

LESSON 14: THE NOUN: ABSOLUTE AND CONSTRUCT

"STATE"

In a previous lesson you learned that the terms gender and number are two concepts which are indicated by various endings of Hebrew nouns. A third term which applies to the function of a Hebrew noun is STATE.

A noun which functions independently of any other word is said to be in ABSOLUTE STATE.

A noun which functions in close connection with another noun is said to be in CONSTRUCT STATE.

The CONSTRUCT STATE of a noun is often a form which exhibits an internal vowel change and which has a special ending to replace an older (original) genitive ending. It is thus a form which is commonly identified in terms of an "of" relationship with the following noun. In addition, the accent will often shift because of the vowel changes undergone by a noun in the CONSTRUCT STATE.

The following chart gives the basic pattern of nouns in CONSTRUCT STATE. Later charts will illustrate particular types of nouns.

סוּס	horse	סוּסָה	mare
סוּס־	the horse of	סוּסַת־	the mare of
סוּסִים	horses	סוּסוֹת	mares
סוּסֵי־	the horses of	סוּסוֹת־	the mares of

In many instances the construct state is joined to the following noun by מַקֵּף (see page 19). This indicates a close relationship between the noun in construct and the noun which immediately follows it. Nothing ever comes between the noun in construct state and its partner, the noun that follows, except a second or third noun in the construct state (see below).

The masculine singular form סוּס shows that a mono-syllabic noun may remain unchanged in its singular form of the construct state.

The יֵ ending of the masculine plural construct is also the dual construct ending of dual nouns.

The תֵ ending of the feminine singular construct is the result of two things. First, long Qameṣ reduces to short Pataḥ. Second, the old feminine ending reappears.

A noun in the construct state does not require the definite article because it is governed by the following noun. That following noun may or may not be articular.

A construct "chain" may consist of more than two nouns together. In such a construction, all nouns except the final one are in the construct state. Cf:

בֵּית־מֶלֶךְ־יִשְׂרָאֵל   the house of the King of Israel

In each of the charts below the order of the words listed will be: absolute singular, construct singular, absolute plural, construct plural.

1. The following chart lists monosyllabic nouns which undergo no change from the singular absolute to the singular construct state. The list is not exhaustive but merely representative.

עַם/עָם	עַם־	עַמִּים	עַמֵּי־	people (m)
אִישׁ	אִישׁ־	אֲנָשִׁים	אַנְשֵׁי־	man (m)
בַּת	בַּת־	בָּנוֹת	בְּנוֹת־	daughter (f)
עִיר	עִיר־	עָרִים	עָרֵי־	city (f)

2. The following chart lists monosyllabic nouns which undergo reduction of a long vowel to a short one in the singular construct.

71

בֵּן	בֶּן־	בָּנִים	בְּנֵי־	son (m)
פַּר	פַּר־	פָּרִים	פָּרֵי־	bull (m)
יָד	יַד־	יָדוֹת	יְדוֹת־	hand (f)
בַּיִת	בֵּית־	בָּתִּים	בָּתֵּי־	house (m)

3. The following chart is a list of representative bisyllabic nouns which undergo long vowel reduction before assuming appropriate endings for the construct state.

דָּבָר	דְּבַר־	דְּבָרִים	דִּבְרֵי־	word (m)
גָּמָל	גְּמַל־	גְּמַלִים	גְּמַלֵי־	camel (m)
חָכָם	חֲכַם־	חֲכָמִים	חַכְמֵי־	wise one (m)
נָבִיא	נְבִיא־	נְבִיאִים	נְבִיאֵי־	prophet (m)
יֶלֶד	יֶלֶד־	יְלָדִים	יַלְדֵי־	boy (m)
מֶלֶךְ	מֶלֶךְ־	מְלָכִים	מַלְכֵי־	king (m)
כּוֹכָב	כּוֹכַב־	כּוֹכָבִים	כּוֹכְבֵי־	star (m)
יַלְדָּה	יַלְדַּת־	יְלָדוֹת	יַלְדוֹת־	girl (f)

EXERCISE

Locate and explain ten construct noun forms in Genesis 22.

READING GENESIS 23:11-15

נתתי   "I have given." Root: נתן.

לָךְ   This is the pausal form of לְךָ.

לְעֵינֵי	"in the presence of." Cf. עַיִן, "an eye."
לִפְנֵי	"before."
אַךְ	"only."
לוּ	A particle which indicates that the verb of the clause is in the subjunctive mood.
שָׁמָּה	"there."
ארבע מאת	"four hundred."
שֶׁקֶל	"a shekel."
ביני ובינך	"between me and you." Cf. בַּיִן, in construct, בֵּין, "between."

Vocabulary Review Lessons 10 - 14

These words should be learned before going on to Lesson 15.

חָכָם	קָבַר	נָגַד	שֶׁבַע
נָבִיא	זֹאת	בְּכוֹר	נְאֻם יְהֹוָה
אַה	עָנָה	יָלַד	כִּי יַעַן
שָׁמָה	נָשִׂיא	פִּילֶגֶשׁ	עָשָׂה
אַרְבַּע	תָּוֶךְ	אֵלֶה	בָּרַח
שֶׁקֶל	מִבְחָר	שָׂרָה	רָבָה
	כָּלָה	חַי	כּוֹכָב
	לֹא	מֵאָה	חוֹל
	שָׁהֹה	עֶשְׂרִים	שָׂפָה
	דָּבָר	שָׁנָה	יָם
	אִם	שֶׁבַע	יָרַשׁ
	יֵשׁ	מוּת	שַׁעַר
	נֶפֶשׁ	בּוֹא	אֹיֵב
	מְעָרָה	סָפַד	זֶרַע
	פֶּגַע	בָּכָה	כֹּל
	קָצֶה	פָּנִי	גּוֹי
	שָׂדֶה	גֵּר	עֵקֶב אֲשֶׁר
	כֶּסֶף	תּוֹשָׁב	שׁוּב
	עַם הָאָרֶץ	נָתַן	קוּם

Review of Pronominal Suffixes with singular nouns is on page 57, plural nouns page 60, and demonstrative pronouns page 65.

LESSON 15: THE QAL IMPERFECT

The first step in learning the Qal Imperfect is to acquire a thorough knowledge of the Qal Perfect. Before you read any more of this lesson, write from memory the conjugation of שמר in the Qal Perfect. If you did not re- member it perfectly, review it until you can write it with ease.

The term "perfect" refers to past, active action, or action which already has been completed (perfected). The term "imperfect" indicates action which has not yet been completed (perfected). It corresponds roughly to English future tense. Note however that when immediately preceded by the letter VAV, an imperfect "form" is often translated by a perfect "meaning." This will be explained fully in a later lesson. Here is a sample conjugation of the Hebrew Qal Imperfect.

אֶשְׁמֹר	I will guard
תִּשְׁמֹר	you (m) will guard
תִּשְׁמְרִי	you (f) will guard
יִשְׁמֹר	he will guard
תִּשְׁמֹר	she will guard
נִשְׁמֹר	we will guard
תִּשְׁמְרוּ	you (m) will guard
תִּשְׁמֹרְנָה	you (f) will guard
יִשְׁמְרוּ	they (m) will guard
תִּשְׁמֹרְנָה	they (f) will guard

OBSERVATIONS ON THE QAL IMPERFECT

The preformative vowel is Ḥireq except in the first person singular, where א takes Seghol.

There is some duplication of form. Second person masculine singular and third person feminine singular are alike as are the plural second and third persons feminine.

Certain preformative consonants are characteristic:

א indicates first person singular.
נ indicates first person plural.
י indicates third person masculine, singular and plural.
ת indicates second person (all forms) as well as third person feminine forms, singular and plural.

These preformatives perform the same function in the Qal Imperfect that the suffix endings perform in the Perfect of the Qal. They indicate tense, person, number, and gender.

The thematic or characteristic vowel is normally a Ḥolem. It becomes Pataḥ in certain cases:

1. If either the second or third letter of the verbal root is a laryngael: יִשְׁמַע he will hear; תִּשְׁלַח she will send.

2. In irregular fashion for certain verbs: יִכְבַּד he will be heavy; יִרְגַּשׁ he will rage.

ACCENTS: NOUNS

The accent or stress in Hebrew pronunciation normally falls on the ultima. The most notable exception is the Segholate noun studied earlier (see pages 30 and 31.)

There are other common words which are not accented on the ultima. They include בַּיִת and לַיְלָה.

ACCENTS: VERBS

The Hebrew verb is normally accented on its second root letter.

נִשְׁמֹר   תִּשְׁמֹרְנָה   שָׁמַרְתִּי   שָׁמַר

But there are two notable exceptions to this rule.

1. When the vowel of the second root letter is a Sheva, simple or compound, the accent shifts to the following syllable.

אָהֲבָה   שָׁמְרָה   שָׁמְרָה   תִּשְׁמְרוּ

2. The second person plural endings of the Perfect always attract the accent.

שְׁמַרְתֶּם   שְׁמַרְתֶּן

LEARNING VOCABULARY

לָבַשׁ	put on clothes	מִדְבָּר	wilderness
קָנָה	acquire, buy	מֶלֶךְ	to be king
בֵּרֵךְ	to bow the knee	גִּבּוֹר	warrior
דֶּרֶךְ	road, way	דֶּלֶת	door
יָטַב	to be good	יָרַשׁ	to possess
כָּתַב	to write	חָלַם	to dream
שֵׁם	a name	אָבַד	to perish
אֶתְמוֹל	yesterday	הַיּוֹם	today
חֲלוֹם	a dream	מָחָר	tomorrow
בְּהֵמָה	cattle		

1. אֶשְׁמֹר אֶת־הַבְּהֵמָה בַּדֶּרֶךְ׃
2. בָּעִיר הַקְּדוֹשָׁה אֶקְנֶה¹ לָהֶם׃
3. אֶת־שֵׁם־הַמָּקוֹם אֶקְרָא² יהוה יִרְאֶה׃
4. אָמַר אַבְרָהָם אֶבְנֶה³ מִזְבֵּחַ׃
5. חָלַם יוֹסֵף חֲלוֹם וְאָמַר הַמַּלְאָךְ תִּמְלֹךְ׃
6. בַּיּוֹם הַהוּא תִּמְלֹךְ שִׁמְעוֹן׃
7. לֵאָה, תִּשְׁמְרִי אֶת־הַדֶּרֶךְ׃
8. בַּמִּדְבָּר יִשְׁמֹר אֶת־הַפָּרִים׃
9. יִכְתּוֹב⁴ בַּסֵּפֶר דְּבָרִים טוֹבִית׃
10. יִלְבַּשׁ בְּגָדִים בַּבֹּקֶר׃
11. בִּירוּשָׁלַיִם בְּגָדִים טוֹבִים׃
12. מָהֳר אֶת־הָאָרֶץ׃
13. הַיּוֹם נִשְׁמֹר אֶת־הָאָרֶץ׃
14. גִּבּוֹרִים אֲנַחְנוּ בַּמִּדְבָּר׃
15. בְּבֵית־הַסֵּפֶר כָּתְבוּ וְקָרְאוּ׃
16. יוֹסֵף וּבִנְיָמִין קָרְאוּ מִן הַסֵּפֶר הַקָּדוֹשׁ׃
17. דָּן וְיוֹסֵף וּבִנְיָמִין הָלְכוּ בַּמִּדְבָּר׃
18. יִשְׁמְרוּ אֶת־הַגִּבּוֹרִים הַחֲזָקִים׃
19. הֵם יְבָרְכוּ אֶת־הַיְלָדִים׃

---

¹Qal Imperfect of קנה

²Qal Imperfect of קרא

³Qal Imperfect of בנה

⁴Alternative to יכתב

וישקל   "and [Abraham] paid."   Root: שקל.

עבר ל   "according to."

סחר   "merchant."   The phrase כסף עבר לסחר means "standard currency."

גבלו   "its boundary."

סביב   "around, surrounding."

מקנה   "a possession."

ואחרי כן   "Then afterwards."

מאת   "from."

LESSON 16: QAL IMPERATIVE, JUSSIVE, AND COHORTATIVE

THE QAL IMPERATIVE

The Hebrew Imperative occurs only in second person forms, singular and plural. It is used to express positive commands and may be described as a shortened form of the Imperfect. The forms of the Imperative are:

	WATCH!	DWELL!
m. sg.	שְׁמֹר	שְׁכַב
f. sg.	שִׁמְרִי	שִׁכְבִי
m. pl.	שִׁמְרוּ	שִׁכְבוּ
f. pl.	שְׁמֹרְנָה	שְׁכַבְנָה

THE QAL JUSSIVE

The term jussive applies to apparently Imperfect second or third person forms which by context are not simple imperfects in <u>meaning</u>. Some words have retained a separate form for the jussive, most have not.

	Imperfect Meaning	Jussive Meaning
תִּשְׁמֹר	you will watch	may you watch
יִשְׁמֹר	he will watch	may he/let him watch

HE COHORTATIVE

The He-Cohortative is an ה- ending added to the first person imperfect form which extends the imperfect meaning to an imperative or to a first person promise or polite command.

Imperfect	אֶשְׁמֹר	I shall watch
	נִשְׁמֹר	we shall watch
Cohortative	אֶשְׁמְרָה	let me watch/I <u>will</u> watch
	נִשְׁמְרָה	let us watch/we <u>will</u> watch

The Cohortative ending takes the stress, reducing preceding Holem to Vocal Sheva.

Note that an ה- ending is often added to a regular imperative form for emphasis. You should be able to recognize such forms in context when they appear in reading.

NEGATIVE COMMANDS OR PROHIBITIONS

Negative commands are expressed with the regular second person imperfect forms preceded by a negative word, either אַל or לֹא.

1. Permanent or unchanging commands are expressed with the imperfect second person and לֹא.

לֹא תִשְׁמֹר	do not watch!	never watch!
לֹא תִשְׁמְרוּ	do not watch!	never watch!
לֹא תִרְצָח	do not murder!	never murder! (Exodus 20:13)

2. Immediate or specific, temporary-situation negatives are expressed with the jussive second or third person singular and אַל.

אַל־תִּשְׁמֹר אֶת־הַפָּרוֹת do not watch the cows (any longer)

אַל־יִשְׁמֹר אֶת־הַפָּרוֹת let him not watch the cows

אַל־תִּקְרָא אֶת־הַסֵּפֶר עַתָּה do not read the book now

LEARNING VOCABULARY

אָהַב	he loved	שָׂנֵא	he hated
שָׁפַט	he judged	מִשְׁפָּט	judgment, justice
פָּנִים	(pl) face, front	לִפְנֵי	before, to the face of
לָקַט	he picked, he gathered up	עָבַד	he served
עֶבֶד	servant, slave	רָדַף	he pursued
אַחֲרֵי	after	עַתָּה	now

READING AND TRANSLATING

1. שְׁמֹר אֶת־הַחֲמוֹר:

2. שִׁמְרוּ אֶת־הַסּוּסִים הַזְּקֵנִים וְהַגְּמַלִים הָרָעִים:

3. לִקְטִי אֶת־הַבְּגָדִים הַזְּקֵנִים:

4. שְׁמֹרְנָה אֶת־הַיְלָדוֹת הַקְּטַנּוֹת בְּבֵית הַזָּקֵן:

5. הָעֶבֶד אָמַר לְאַבְרָהָם אֶשְׁמְרָה אֶת־הַחֲמוֹרִים:

6. אָמַר יְהוּדָה לְאַבְרָהָם אֶרְדְּפָה אַחֲרֵי הָאֲנָשִׁים:

7. אָמְרוּ רָחֵל וְלֵאָה נִלְקְטָה אֶת־הַבְּגָדִים:

8. אַל תִּשְׁפֹּט אֶת־הָאִישׁ הָרַע:

9. אַל תִּשְׁמְעוּ לְקוֹל הָאִישׁ הַזָּקֵן:

10. לֹא תִשְׂנָא לֹא תִרְצַח תִּרְדּוֹף אַחֲרֵי נָשִׁים רָעוֹת:

82

בָא — "he was going." Root: בּוֹא.

בֵּרֵךְ — "[and Yahweh] blessed." This root, ברך, occurs almost exclusively in the Piel [intensive] conjugation. In the Qal, it means to bend the knee or to bow. In the Piel, it means to bless.

זְקַן בֵּיתוֹ — "the old one in his house."

הַמּשֵׁל — "the ruler of." Or, "the one who ruled." This construction combines the article with a Qal active participle to be sutdied later.

שִׂים נָא — "place now." שִׂים is a Qal imperative second person singular masculine form in this context. It is also the spelling of the infinitive construct of the verb. נָא is a postpositive particle of entreaty. Used with imperatives, jussives, cohortatives, and some conjunctions and interjections, it means "please" or "I entreat." It does not inflect.

יְרֵכִי — "my thigh." Cf. יָרֵךְ thigh.

וְאַשְׁבִּיעֲךָ — "And I will cause you to swear." אַשְׁבִּיעַ is a Hiphil imperfect form of שבע.

לֹא תִקַּח — "you will not take." Qal imperfect from לקח.

הַכְּנַעֲנִי — "The Canaanites." A singular form with a collective meaning. The י- ending is not a pronominal suffix, but what is called a "gentilic" ending. It makes "Canaanite" from the noun כְּנַעַן, Canaan.

מוֹלַדְתִּי — "my kinfolk." Cf. מוֹלֶדֶת kin, consanguinity.

תֵלֵךְ — "you will go." Imperfect form of הלך.

תֹאבֶה — "she will [not] be willing/agree." Qal imperfect form of אבה.

לָלֶכֶת — "to go." לָ not לְ since it precedes a stressed syllable. לֶכֶת is the Qal infinitive construct of הלך.

הֲהָשֵׁב אשיב   "Should I bring back?" הֲ is an alternate spelling for the interrogative marker הַ. הָשֵׁב is a Hiphil infinitive absolute from שׁוּב which means to return in the Qal but to bring back or to cause someone else to return in the Hiphil. אָשִׁיב is a Hiphil Imperfect of שׁוּב.

הִשָּׁמֶר לך   "be careful." A Niphal imperative form of שׁמר.

פֶּן   "lest."

תָּשִׁיב   "you bring back [my son]." A Hiphil form of שׁוּב. What is the difference between the form תשיב which occurs in this verse and the form אשיב which occurs in verse 5?

שָׁמָּה   שָׁם with mem doubled and adverbial ending ָה.

84

LESSON 17: QAL INFINITIVES

THE QAL INFINITIVE CONSTRUCT

Infinitive construct is the term applied to the more common of the two Hebrew infinitives. In form, it is often the same as the second person masculine singular imperative. It normally occurs following the preposition ל, and this is often comparable to the English infinitive. As a "verbal noun," the Hebrew infinitive construct functions at times as a verb and at other times as a noun. Here are examples of common ways in which the infinitive construct functions.

1. Similar to the English infinitive.

    הִיא אֹבָה לָלֶכֶת: She is willing to go.

2. Similar to the English gerund.

    לִשְׁפֹּט עֲבוֹדָה קָשָׁה: Judging is hard work.

3. With an object.

    לִשְׁמֹר צֹאן עֲבוֹדָה קָשָׁה: Watching sheep is hard work.

4. With a subject in the objective case.

    בִּשְׁפֹּט אַבְרָהָם: When Abraham judged.

5. With a pronoun subject suffixed.

    שָׁמְרִי צֹאן עֲבוֹדָה קָשָׁה: My watching sheep is hard work.

    Note the special form of the infinitive to which a suffix is added: שָׁמְר-.

6. With a suffixed object.

יָשַׁב אַבְרָהָם לְשָׁמְרוֹ׃   Abraham sat to watch him.

THE QAL INFINITIVE ABSOLUTE

Hebrew uses a second type of infinitive for certain grammatical functions. The infinitive absolute takes the following forms:

שָׁמוֹעַ   שָׁפוֹט   שָׁמוֹר

In function, the infinitive absolute has several different usages.

1. When it immediately precedes its cognate verb, it expresses intensity or emphasis.

שָׁמוֹר שָׁמַר   He indeed/really watched.

שָׁמוֹר יִשְׁמֹר   He will indeed watch.

2. When it immediately follows its cognate verb, it expresses duration or continuation.

שָׁמַר שָׁמוֹר   He watched continually.

יִשְׁמֹר שָׁמוֹר   He will watch continually.

Note that both uses of the infinitive absolute so far illustrated are foreign to English expression. In both cases a good translator will try first to understand the impact of the Hebrew idiom and then render it into acceptable English. No hard, fixed rule of equivalency can be followed for every case.

3. The infinitive absolute is sometimes used as a surrogate for the imperative.

שָׁמוֹר אֶת־יוֹם הַשַּׁבָּת׃   Keep the day of Sabbath!

Note that the infinitive absolute does not inflect, does not take suffixes, and is never preceded by a preposition.

EXERCISE

Carefully study the words listed below. Be prepared
to identify them as infinitive construct, infinitive absolute,
or not an infinitive at all.

11. שְׁפֹט	6. לְקֹוט	1. שָׁמֹר
12. שָׁאֹוב	7. שָׁמֹור	2. שְׁמֹעַ
13. עֲמֹוד	8. יִשְׁמֹור	3. שָׁמֹועַ
14. לְקֹט	9. עָמֹוד	4. שָׁמֹועַ
15. יֹושֵׁב	10. שְׁחֹט	5. שֹׁמֵר

READING AND TRANSLATING

1. אַבְרָהָם הָלַךְ אֶל הָהָר וְשָׁחֹוט שָׁחַט אֶת־הָאָיִל:

2. הָלַךְ הָלֹוךְ אַבְרָהָם אֶל הָהָר לִשְׁחֹט אֶת־בְּנֹו:

3. בִּשְׁפֹט יִצְחָק אֶת־הָאִישׁ הַהוּא עָבַד בָּעִיר:

4. עַל שָׁמְרָם אֶת־הַיֶּלֶד הֵם לֹא מָצְאוּ כָסֶף:

5. אָמַר אַבְרָהָם לָעֶבֶד לִשְׁמֹר אֶת־הַגְּמַלִּים כֹּל־הַלָּיְלָה (night):

6. אָמְרָה שָׂרָה לַנַּעֲרָה לִמְצֹא אֶת הַיֶּלֶד הַקָּטֹן:

7. תִּשְׁמֹור שָׁמֹור הַנַּעֲרָה אֶת הַיֶּלֶד הַקָּטֹן כֹּל־הַיֹּום:

8. שָׁמֹור שָׁמְרוּ הַנְּעָרֹות אֶת־הַיְלָדֹות:

9. שָׁמֹור תִּשְׁמֹרְנָה הַנְּעָרֹות אֶת־הַיְלָדֹות בַּבָּיִת:

READING GENESIS 24:7-12

אֶתֵּן   "I will give." Root: נתן.

לקחת	Translate this perfect form in the future.
תאבה	"[If the lady is not] willing. Root: אבה.
נקית	"you will be relieved." Root: נקה.
תשב	"do [not] bring."
רק	"only."
שמה	"[to] there." The ה added to the common word שם is called He-Locative (see next lesson). It is an old accusative-like ending which in early Hebrew expressed the idea of "motion toward."
וישם	"then he placed." Root: שִׂים.
וישבע	"and he took an oath." Niphal form of שבע.
על	"about, regarding."
עשרה	"ten." This is the masculine form.
וילך	"and he went." Root: הלך.
טוב	"good things."
ארם נהרים	"Mesopotamia."
ויברך	"Then he made [the camels] kneel." This is a Hiphil form of ברך.
מחוץ ל	"outside."
אל	In this context, "near."
באר	"the well of." בְּאֵר is also the lexical form of this word.
מים	"water." Note the dual ending for this very common collective noun. It always takes its modifiers in the masculine plural form. Cf. מַיִם קָרִים "cold water."
לעת ערב	"at evening time." Lexical forms: עֵת, time; עֶרֶב, evening.

צאת   "the appearance of." צאת is actually an infinitive construct form of יצא which means to
go forth, to exit. Here the infinitive construct is used as a noun, and refers to that
time in the evening when the young ladies of
the village would go out to draw water.

השאבת   "the [water] drawers." Cf. שאב to draw
[water]. This form is a Qal active participle,
feminine plural.

הקרה נא   "Please act."

לפני   "for me." I.e., in my presence.

היום   "today."

עשה   "do!"

חסד   "covenant faithfulness."

LESSON 18: THE QAL ACTIVE PARTICIPLE

THE FORM OF THE QAL ACTIVE PARTICIPLE

The Qal Participle exhibits both active and passive (see next lesson) forms in regular (non-stative) verbs. Its form may be masculine or feminine, singular or plural, just like the forms of nouns and adjectives learned above. Here is the Qal Active Participle:

	Singular	Plural
Masc.	שׁוֹמֵר	שׁוֹמְרִים
Fem.	שׁוֹמְרָה/שׁוֹמֶ֫רֶת	שׁוֹמְרוֹת

THE MAIN USES OF THE PARTICIPLE

The Hebrew participle is a verbal form which functions at times like a verb and at times like an adjective. Hence, it is called a "verbal adjective."

1. As the verb of a clause or sentence, it must have an expressed subject.

הָאִישׁ שׁוֹמֵר אֶת־הַגָּמָל׃	The man is watching the camel.
הָאֲנָשִׁים שׁוֹמְרִים אֶת־הַגָּמָל׃	The men are watching the camel.
הָאִשָּׁה שׁוֹמֶ֫רֶת אֶת־הַיֶּ֫לֶד׃	The woman is watching the boy.
הַנָּשִׁים שׁוֹמְרוֹת אֶת־הַיֶּ֫לֶד׃	The women are watching the boy.

Note that the participle agrees with its subject in number and gender.

90

2. As an attributive, the participle is like the adjective and functions as an appostiive.

הָאִישׁ הַשׁוֹמֵר אֶת־הַגָּמָל   The man [who is] watching the camel.

הָאֲנָשִׁים הַשׁוֹמְרִים אֶת־הַגָּמָל   The men [who are] watching the camel.

3. As a substantive, the participle is again like the adjective which is substantive, and functions as a noun.

הַשׁוֹמֵר אֶת־הַסּוּסִים   The one who watches the horses.

הַשּׁוֹאֲבוֹת אֶת־הַמַּיִם   The water-drawers; the ones (f.) who draw water.

4. Note that the Hebrew participle has no <u>tense</u> of its own, but follows that of the main verb in the clause.

EXERCISES

Write the Qal active participle for each of the following words: שָׁמַר, שָׁפַט, יָשַׁב, שָׁמַע, יָרַד .

Identify the following forms according to number, gender, and voice:

1. אוֹהֶבֶת		6. עוֹמֵד		11. יוֹצְאִים	
2. קוֹרְאִים		7. שׁוֹלְחִים		12. שׁוֹמֵר	
3. כּוֹתְבוֹת		8. שׁוֹפְטִים		13. שׁוֹמֵעַ	
4. שׁוֹמֶּרֶת		9. שׁוֹמְעָה		14. שׁוֹאֲבָה	
5. לֹקֵט		10. קוֹרְאוֹת		15. יוֹרֶדֶת	

THE HE-LOCATIVE

The suffix הָ‍ may be added to a noun (common or proper) or to an adverb to indicate "motion toward." Note the following facts about the He-Locative:

a. The suffix is never accented, and should not be confused with the feminine singular ending.

91

b. The common noun may or may not have the article.

c. Certain rather unpredictable vowel changes occur in a word to which He-Locative is added. These changes should be observed and memorized for each word.

   Below are examples of He-Locative. Note carefully the accents!

1. With common nouns:

אַ֫רְצָה	to the ground
הַשָּׁמַ֫יְמָה	heavenward
הָעִ֫ירָה	toward the city
הָעַ֫יְנָה	toward the well
[הַ]בַּ֫יְתָה	homeward, to the house
הָהָ֫רָה	mountainward
מִדְבָּ֫רָה	toward the wilderness

2. With proper nouns:

מִצְרַ֫יְמָה	toward Egypt
יְרוּשָׁלַ֫יְמָה	toward Jerusalem
שְׁאֹ֫לָה	toward Sheol
נֶ֫גְבָּה	toward the Negev
אַ֫רְצָה כְּנַ֫עַן	toward the land of Canaan

3. With directional adverbs:

שָׁ֫מָּה	thither, to there
הֵ֫נָּה	hither, to here
אָ֫נָה	whither?, to where?

4. With the four directions: יָם, קֶ֫דֶם, תֵּימָן, צָפוֹן.

צָפ֫וֹנָה	northward
תֵּימָ֫נָה	southward
קֵ֫דְמָה	eastward
יָ֫מָּה	westward, seaward

READING AND TRANSLATING

1. הָעֶבֶד הוֹלֵךְ אֲרַם נַהֲרָיְמָה:

2. הַהוֹלְכִים אֶל־אֲרַם נַהֲרַיִם שָׁמוֹר שָׁמְרוּ אֶת־הַדָּרֶךְ:

3. הַמֶּלֶךְ הֶחָכָם מוֹלֵךְ עַל־יִשְׂרָאֵל:

4. הַמֶּלֶךְ הַמּוֹלֵךְ עַל־יִשְׂרָאֵל שָׁפוֹט יִשְׁפּוֹט אֶת הָאֲנָשִׁים הָרָעִים:

5. מְלָכִים חֲזָקִים מֹלְכִים עַל־אֲרָצוֹת רַבּוֹת:

6. הַמְּלָכִים הַמּוֹלְכִים עַל אֲרָצוֹת רַבּוֹת שָׁלְחוּ אֲנָשִׁים רַבִּים אֲרַם נַהֲרָיְמָה:

7. הַנַּעֲרָה יוֹשֶׁבֶת בְּחֶבְרוֹן:

8. הַנַּעֲרָה הַיּוֹשֶׁבֶת בְּחֶבְרוֹן קָרְאָה מִן הַסֵּפֶר הַטּוֹב לַיְלָדִים הַקְּטַנִּים:

9. הָעֲבָדוֹת הַיּשְׁבוֹת בְּחֶבְרוֹן קָרְאוּ מִן הַסֵּפֶר הַקָּדוֹשׁ:

10. הָעֲבָדוֹת הַזְּקֵנוֹת יוֹשְׁבוֹת בָּעִיר:

READING GENESIS 24:13-18

נצב   "[I] am stationed/standing/." A Niphal participle masculine singular from נצב.

עין   Construct state of עַיִן, a well, fountain.

והיה   "So let it come to pass/happen/be."

אמר   "I shall say."

הטי   "let down." Lit., "stretch out." Hiphil imperative, feminine singular. Root: נטה.

כדך   "your jar." Cf. כַּד, a jar, vessel.

שתה   "drink!" Form _____? Root _____?

אשקה   "I will water." Hiphil imperfect of שקה.

אתה   "her." Used as the direct object.

הכחת   "you have decided." Hiphil perfect of יכח.

93

טרם   "before." An adverb, not a preposition.

כלה   "he finished."

לדבר   "speaking." Piel infinitive of דבר, used like an English gerund (see page 86).

ילדה   "was born." Pual of ילד.

אשת   "the wife of." Construct state of אִשָּׁה.

שכמה   "her shoulder." Lexical form: שְׁכֶם.

ידעה   Read יָדַע with suffix "her."

ותרד   "and she descended." Root: ירד.

ותמלא   "and filled." In the Piel, the Stative Verb assumes an active meaning.

ותעל   "and she came up," i.e., from the well.

וירץ   "then [the servant] ran." Root: רוּץ.

לקראתה   "to meet her."

הגמיאיני   "give me a drink." Hiphil imperative of גמא.

מעט   "a little."

ותמהר   "Then she hurried. Piel form of מהר.

ותרד   "and let down." Hiphil form of ירד.

ותשקהו   "and she gave him a drink." Lit., "she watered him." Root: שקה.

LESSON 19: THE QAL PASSIVE PARTICIPLE,

SOME COMMON NOUNS

THE QAL PASSIVE PARTICIPLE

Forms of the Qal Passive Participle show a declension similar to that of the Qal Active Participle studied in the last lesson. However, the inner vocalization is different. Observe:

	Singular	Plural
Masc.	שָׁמוּר	שְׁמוּרִים
Fem.	שְׁמוּרָה	שְׁמוּרוֹת

The functions of the passive participle are similar to those of the active participle:

הַדָּבָר שָׁמוּר   The matter is guarded.

הַדָּבָר הַשָּׁמוּר   The matter which is guarded.

THE QAL STATIVE PARTICIPLE

The stative verbs obviously cannot form active or passive participles in the Qal. The stative participle is merely an adjective, as the verb כבד shows. The verbal

95

form כָּבֵד, "he was heavy," becomes the adjective "heavy." Cf.

כְּבֵדוֹת   כְּבֵדִים   כְּבֵדָה   כָּבֵד

EXERCISES

Write the Qal Passive Participle forms for each of the following words:

לקט   נתן   שמר   כתב

Translate the following sentences into English and then rewrite them, substituting different forms of the verb for the Qal passive participles which each one contains.

1.   הַדָּבָר שָׁמוּעַ בַּהֵיכָל:

2.   הַדָּבָר הַשָּׁמוּעַ בַּהֵיכָל כָּתוּב בְּסֵפֶר גָּדוֹל:

3.   הַדְּבָרִים מִן הַמֶּלֶךְ קְרוּאִים לְעַם־יִשְׂרָאֵל:

4.   הַדְּבָרִים הַקְּרוּאִים לְיִשְׂרָאֵל כְּתוּבִים בַּסֵּפֶר הַקָּדוֹשׁ:

FAMILIAR NOUNS WITH UNUSUAL FORMS

The following words are the familiar, family-relationship type nouns. Some have been listed in previous charts, others have not. They are listed below for completeness and for ready reference.

אָב	אֲבִי־	אָבוֹת	אֲבוֹת־
אֵם	אֵם־	[אִמּוֹת]	אִמּוֹת־[
בֵּן	בֶּן־	בָּנִים	בְּנֵי־
בַּת	בַּת־	בָּנוֹת	בְּנוֹת־
אָח	אֲחִי־	אַחִים	אֲחֵי־
אָחוֹת	אֲחוֹת־		

אִישׁ   אִישׁ־   אֲנָשִׁים   אַנְשֵׁי־

אִשָּׁה   אֵשֶׁת־   נָשִׁים   נְשֵׁי־

NOTES

1. The plural form אבות should simply be noted and memorized. Any explanation of the reason for the form is conjecture.

2. On the construct singular forms אבי and אחי, see page 60.

3. אחות is an appropriation of the plural form for a singular function. Modern Hebrew uses the plural אֲחָיוֹת, but in the Bible this plural is not found without a suffix.

THE DUAL CONSTRUCT

The dual construct is the same as the masculine plural construct. The following chart is given for convenience. If you do not know the meaning of any word in this chart or the one above, look it up in the Glossary and memorize it.

עַיִן   עֵין־   עֵינַיִם   עֵינַי־

אֹזֶן   אֹזֶן־   אָזְנַיִם   אָזְנַי־

יָד   יַד־   יָדַיִם   יָדַי־

רֶגֶל   רֶגֶל־   רַגְלַיִם   רַגְלַי־

אַף   [אַף־]   אַפַּיִם   [אַפַּי־]

פָּנֶה   [פָּנֶה]   פָּנִים   פָּנַי־

פֶּה   פִּי־   פִּיּוֹת   [פִּיּוֹת]

מַיִם   מֵי/מֵימֵי־

שָׁמַיִם   שְׁמֵי־

NOTES

1. עַיִן meaning "eye" occurs only in the dual. Cf. עֵינֹת עַיִן, a fountain or well, in Genesis 24:13.

2. יָד (see page 35) and רגל (see page 35) occur in both dual and plural forms.

3. The forms in brackets do not occur in the Hebrew Bible but are reconstructed on the analogy of similar forms.

4. פֶּה, "mouth," is included to complete the list of words which refer to the face or some part of it.

5. מַיִם and שמים are dual in spelling but collective or plural in meaning. They may be termed duals or plurals of "extent."

READING GENESIS 24:19-25

ותכל   "when she had finished." Root: כלה.

להשקתו   "giving him a drink." A Hiphil infinitive construct from שקה plus a suffix.

עד אם   "until."

כלו   "they have finished." Piel form of כלה.

לשתת   "drinking." A Qal infinitive construct of שתה.

ותער   "and she emptied." Root: ערה.

שקת   "water-trough."

ותשאב   Translate this imperfect form in the past tense.

משתאה   "was gazing at her." Root: שאה.

מחריש   "silently."

לדעת   This is the Qal infinitive construct of ידע.

הַהִצְלִיחַ   "did [Yahweh] make successful?" The first ה is a question mark. The verbal form is a Hiphil, from the root צלח.

נזם   "a nose ring."

בקע   "half."

משקלו   "its weight." Lexical form: מִשְׁקָל.

צמידים   "bracelets." Singular: צָמִיד.

הגידי   "tell!" Hiphil imperative, feminine singular. Root: נגד.

ללין   "to spend the night."

תבן   "straw."

מספוא   "fodder."

לון   An alternate form of לין.

LESSON 20: THE QAL STATIVE

THE STATIVE VERB

The Hebrew verb called "stative" indicates a state-of-being in contrast to the active verb which indicates a kind of action or motion.

Normally, the stative verbs take either Ṣere or dot Ḥolem as a thematic vowel, or the vowel used by the lexical form. However, some statives retain Pataḥ, as the charts below indicate. Before studying כבד, קטן, and שכב, reread and carefully review all forms of שמר which have been given previously.

PERFECT

כָּבַדְתִּי	קָטֹנְתִּי	שָׁכַבְתִּי
כָּבַדְתָּ	קָטֹנְתָּ	שָׁכַבְתָּ
כָּבַדְתְּ	קָטֹנְתְּ	שָׁכַבְתְּ
כָּבֵד	קָטֹן	שָׁכַב
כָּבְדָה	קָטְנָה	שָׁכְבָה
כָּבַדְנוּ	קָטֹנּוּ	שָׁכַבְנוּ
כְּבַדְתֶּם	קְטָנְתֶּם	שְׁכַבְתֶּם
כְּבַדְתֶּן	קְטָנְתֶּן	שְׁכַבְתֶּן
כָּבְדוּ	קָטְנוּ	שָׁכְבוּ

IMPERFECT

אֶכְבַּד	אֶקְטַן	אֶשְׁכַּב
תִּכְבַּד	תִּקְטַן	תִּשְׁכַּב
תִּכְבְּדִי	תִּקְטְנִי	תִּשְׁכְּבִי
יִכְבַּד	יִקְטַן	יִשְׁכַּב
תִּכְבַּד	תִּקְטַן	תִּשְׁכַּב
נִכְבַּד	נִקְטַן	נִשְׁכַּב
תִּכְבְּדוּ	תִּקְטְנוּ	תִּשְׁכְּבוּ
תִּכְבַּדְנָה	תִּקְטַנָּה	תִּשְׁכַּבְנָה
יִכְבְּדוּ	יִקְטְנוּ	יִשְׁכְּבוּ
תִּכְבַּדְנָה	תִּקְטַנָּה	תִּשְׁכַּבְנָה

NOTES

1. קטן exhibits some unusual forms because of the presence of the final ן. Cf. those forms in which the d.l. indicates a doubled letter Nun. The first belongs to the root, the other belongs to the ending.

2. In the second person plural forms of the perfect, note that the Qames is Qames Ḥatuph.

3. Note the thematic vowel Pataḥ for stative verbs in the Imperfect.

4. The following stative verbs may be conjugated according to the patterns given above:

זָקֵן, יִזְקַן   רָעֵב, יִרְעַב   גָּדֵל, יִגְדַּל   צָמֵא, יִצְמָא

שָׁכֵל, יִשְׁכַּל   שָׁכֵן, יִשְׁכַּן

101

LEARNING VOCABULARY

רָעֵב	he was hungry	צָמֵא	he was thirsty
שָׁכֹל	he was bereaved (of children)	שָׁכַב, שָׁכֵב	he lay down
שָׁכֵן	he dwelt, lay down	גָּדַל	he was great
זָקֵן	he was old	כָּבֵד	he was rich, respected, it was heavy
קָטֹן	he was small, young, unimportant		

EXERCISE

1. אַבְרָהָם זָקֵן וְהָלַךְ אֶל־יְרוּשָׁלַיִם עִם יִצְחָק:

2. שָׂרָה זָקְנָה וְהָלְכָה אֶל־בֵּית־לֶחֶם עִם לֵאָה:

3. יִגְדְּלוּ הַנְּעָרִים הָעֲשִׁירִים בְּמִצְרַיִם:

4. אָמַר אַבְרָהָם לְיִצְחָק גָּדַלְתִּי בְּעִיר קְטַנָּה:

5. גָּדַלְתֶּן בְּהֵיכָל בִּירוּשָׁלָיִם:

6. רָעֲבוּ הַיְלָדִים לְלֶחֶם וְצָמְאוּ לְמָיִם:

7. יוֹסֵף וְיִצְחָק שָׁכְבוּ בְּבֵית־לֶחֶם:

8. אַחֲרֵי כֵן שָׁמְרוּ הַנְּעָרִים אֶת־הַסּוּסִים:

READING GENESIS 24:26-32

וַיִּקֹּד   "So he bowed his head." Root: קדד.

בָּרוּךְ   "blessed." Root _____? Form _____?

אדוני   "my master." Lexical form: אָדוֹן.

עזב   "he did [not] forsake."

אמתו   "his truth." Lexical form: אֱמֶת.

נחני   "[Yahweh] guided me." Root: נחה.

ותרץ   "So [the girl] ran." Root: רוץ.

ותגד   "and told." Root: נגד.

אל   "near."

כראת   "when [he] saw." Prefix כ plus Qal infinitive construct of ראה.

כה   "thus."

דבר   "spoke." Piel form of דבר.

ויבא   "Then he went." Root: בּוֹא.

על   "near."

בוא   "Come!" Qal imperative, second person masculine singular.

פניתי   "I have prepared." Root: פנה.

ויפתח   "Then he unburdened/unloaded." Piel form of פתח.

ויתן   "and he gave." Root: נתן.

לרחץ   "to wash."

אתו   "with him."

REVIEW LESSON IV

Vocabulary Review Lessons 15 - 20

These words should be learned before going on to Lesson 21.

לָבַשׁ	פָּנִים	יָצָא	בָּקַע
קָנָה	לָקַט	שָׁאַב	מִשְׁקָל
בֵּרֵךְ	עָבַד	חֶסֶד	צָמִיד
דֶּרֶךְ	אַחֲרֵי	נִצָּב	לִין
יָטַב	שָׂנֵא	נָטָה	תֶּבֶן
כָּתַב	מִשְׁפָּט	פַּד	מִסְפּוֹא
שֵׁם	עָבַד	שָׁקָה	
אֶתְמוֹל	רָדַף	יָכַח	
חֲלוֹם	עַתָּה	טֶרֶם	
בְּהֵמָה	מָשַׁל	פָּלָה	
מִדְבָּר	שִׂים נָא	שְׁכֶם	
מֶלֶךְ	יָרֵךְ	יָדַע	
גִּבּוֹר	לָקַח	יָרַד	
דֶּלֶת	מוֹלֶדֶת	מָלֵא	
עוֹלָם	אָבָה	רוּץ	
אָבַד	פֶּן	גָּמָא	
מָזֹר	נָקָה	מְעַט	
עָבַר	רַק	מָהַר	
סָגַר	עֶשְׂרֵה	עַד אִם	
גְּבוּל	אֲרַם נַהֲרַיִם	עָרָה	
סָבִיב	חוּץ	שָׁקַט	
מִקְנֶה	בְּאֵר	שָׁאָה	
אָהַב	עֵת	צָלַח	
שָׁפַט	עֶרֶב	נֶזֶם	

Review Of Pronominal Elements In

Various Morphological Situations

For suffixes with the verbs, see the chart, Pronominal Suffixes With The Verb.

	Sing. 1st c.	2nd m.	2nd f.	3rd m.	3rd f.	Plural 1st c.	2nd m.	2nd f.	3rd m.	3rd f.
Suff. c. pl. nouns	ַי	ֶיךָ	ַיִךְ	ָיו	ֶיהָ	ֵינוּ	ֵיכֶם	ֵיכֶן	ֵיהֶם	ֵיהֶן
Suff. c. sep. prep.	ִי	ְךָ	ֵךְ	וֹ	ָהּ	ֵנוּ	ְכֶם	ְכֶן	ָם	ָן
Suff. c. sing. nouns.	ִי	ְךָ	ֵךְ	וֹ	ָהּ	ֵנוּ	ְכֶם	ְכֶן	ָם	ָן
Suff. c. ins. prep.	ִי	ְךָ	ֵךְ	וֹ	ָהּ	ָנוּ	ְכֶם	ְכֶן	ָם	ָן
Pref. c. Impf.	אֶ	תִּ	תִּ	יִ	תִּ	נִ	תִּ ..וּ	תִּ ..נָה	יִ ..וּ	תִּ ..נָה
Aff. c. Perf.	תִּי	תָּ	תְּ		ָה	נוּ	תֶּם	תֶּן	וּ	
Ind. Pers. Pron.	אֲנִי / אָנֹכִי	אַתָּה	אַתְּ	הוּא	הִיא	אֲנַחְנוּ / נַחְנוּ	אַתֶּם	אַתֶּנָּה / אַתֵּן	הֵם / הֵמָּה	הֵן / הֵנָּה

105

	Perfect	Imperfect	Imperative	Cohortative
Sing. 1st c.	שָׁמַרְתִּי	אֶשְׁמֹר		אֶשְׁמְרָה
2nd m.	שָׁמַרְתָּ	תִּשְׁמֹר	שְׁמֹר	
2nd f.	שָׁמַרְתְּ	תִּשְׁמְרִי	שִׁמְרִי	
3rd m.	שָׁמַר	יִשְׁמֹר		
3rd f.	שָׁמְרָה	תִּשְׁמֹר		
Plur. 1st c.	שָׁמַרְנוּ	נִשְׁמֹר		נִשְׁמְרָה
2nd m.	שְׁמַרְתֶּם	תִּשְׁמְרוּ	שִׁמְרוּ	
2nd f.	שְׁמַרְתֶּן	תִּשְׁמֹרְנָה	שְׁמֹרְנָה	
3rd m.	שָׁמְרוּ	יִשְׁמְרוּ		
3rd f.	שָׁמְרוּ	תִּשְׁמֹרְנָה		
Inf. Constr.	שְׁמֹר(ל)			
Inf. Abs.	שָׁמוֹר			

	M. Sing.	F. Sing.	M. Plural	F. Plural
Part. Act.	שׁוֹמֵר	שׁוֹמֶרֶת / שׁוֹמְרָה	שׁוֹמְרִים	שׁוֹמְרוֹת
Part. Pass.	שָׁמוּר	שְׁמוּרָה	שְׁמוּרִים	שְׁמוּרוֹת

LESSON 21: THE VAV-CONSECUTIVE, "WHEN" CLAUSES

THE VAV-CONSECUTIVE

Hebrew uses the VAV for more than purposes of connection or conjunction. It is also used in narrative to change the tense of verbs. That is, it changes a perfect <u>form</u> to an imperfect <u>meaning</u>, and vice versa. When a VAV functions in this manner, it is called "VAV-CONSECUTIVE."

1. With perfect forms, the spelling of Vav is וְ:

וְשָׁמַר אֶת הַפָּרִים מָחָר׃   And he will watch the bulls tomorrow.

Note that the word מָחָר, "tomorrow," rules out the possibility of translating the Vav as a simple connective.

2. With imperfect forms, Vav-Consecutive becomes וַיִּ, using Patah and doubling the preformative letter of the following verb.

וַיִּשְׁמֹר אֶת־הַבָּקָר בַּשָּׂדֶה׃   And he watched the herd in the field.

3. The Vav-Consecutive with a Perfect form often repels the accent. This is particularly true in the case of second person masculine singular forms.

וְיָדַעְתָּ   and you will know;   וְשָׁמַרְתָּ   and you will keep

4. The Vav-Consecutive changes its spelling in the same ways described for Vav-Connective (see pages 36-37).

5. With the first person singular Imperfect, Vav-Consecutive is spelled וָ.

וָאֹמַר   and I said;   יָדַעְתִּי וָאֶשְׁמֹר   I knew and I kept

107

6. With some Imperfect forms, the Vav-Consecutive tends to attract the accent toward itself.

וַיֹּאמֶר and he said

7. Nothing may occur between the Vav and the verb if the form is to be considered a Vav-Consecutive.

שָׁפַט וְלֹא שָׁמַר he judged but he did not keep

8. A common form in narrative is וַיְהִי, "and it came to pass, happened." Because the form is so common, the d.f. is not necessary. Note that יְהִי is a shortened form of יִהְיֶה, the imperfect of היה. Note also that Vav-Consecutive often occurs with shortened forms of the imperfect (see lesson 33).

"WHEN"

The temporal idea of when is expressed in Hebrew by the combination of בּ or כּ and the infinitive construct, or by כאשר with a perfect form.

Note that the phrase, "and it came to pass when the servant of Abraham heard," may be expressed in three different ways:

וַיְהִי כַּאֲשֶׁר שָׁמַע עֶבֶד־אַבְרָהָם

וַיְהִי כִּשְׁמוֹעַ עֶבֶד אַבְרָהָם

וַיְהִי בִּשְׁמוֹעַ עֶבֶד אַבְרָהָם

READING GENESIS 24:33-40

וַיּוּשַׂם   "Then [food] was set." A Hophal imperfect form of שִׂים.

אֹכַל   "I will [not] eat." Qal imperfect form of אכל.

עַד אִם   "until."

דִּבַּרְתִּי   "I have spoken." Piel perfect form of דבר.

דבר   "Speak!" Piel imperative, second person masculine singular. Root: דבר.

וַיֹּאמֶר   Here the fact that direct speech follows immediately after the verb causes an accent shift to the final syllable.

ברך   "has blessed."

שפחת   "hand-maidens." Lexical form: שִׁפְחָה.

ותלד   "And [Sarah] bore." Root: ילד.

זקנתה   "[after] she became old." Combination of זִקְנָה, "oldness," and a suffix, "her."

וישבעני   "Then [my master] made me take an oath."

תקח   Qal imperfect of לקח.

אם לא   In the context of oath-taking, this phrase becomes an emphatic "but" or "indeed."

תלך   Qal imperfect of הלך.

משפחתי   Lexical form: מִשְׁפָּחָה, a family.

התהלכתי   "I have lived." A Hitpael form of הלך.

אתך   "with you." Note that the pausal form has caused the vowel to be lengthened.

הצליח   "he will make prosperous." Hiphil perfect form of צלח.

LESSON 22: THE NIPHAL CONJUGATION

Thus far in your Hebrew studies you have encountered only the Qal stem. Qal, the light, the unencumbered stem of the verb, is the primary conjugation in Hebrew in a dual way. First, it occurs far more frequently in biblical Hebrew than any of the other conjugations. Second, it is the Qal upon which the other stems are based in form and from the Qal that they are derived. To understand the derived stems, you must be certain that you understand fully the Qal conjugation.

THE FUNCTION OF THE NIPHAL

1. The Niphal is either the passive or reflexive of the Qal. שָׁבַר, "he broke;" נִשְׁבַּר, "he was broken."

2. The Niphal is the passive or reflexive of either the Piel or the Hiphil stems of certain verbs.

3. The Niphal may express a state, a condition, or a feeling which involves the subject [compare the Greek middle voice]. Note the Niphal form נִכְמַר, "he grew hot."

THE FORM OF THE NIPHAL

1. The Niphal Perfect is characterized by the presence of the preformative letter נ. Then, the endings of the regular Qal Perfect are added.

2. The Niphal Imperfect uses the same preformative

110

letters employed in the Qal Imperfect. Then, the נ of the Niphal assimilates to the first consonant of the verbal root. That letter is in turn doubled to signal the loss of the נ before it. Thus,

יִנְשָׁמֵר becomes יִשָּׁמֵר.

3. In the Niphal Imperfect, if the first of the three root consonants is a laryngael or ר, which cannot be doubled, the vowel under the preformative letter lengthens to Sere. Thus,

יִעְזֵב becomes יֵעָזֵב.

4. To the characteristic נ of the Niphal, the infinitives and imperatives prefix a secondary ה. As a consequence, the following נ again assimilates. The first of the root letters is accordingly once again doubled to signal the loss of the נ before it.

5. For basic Niphal forms of irregular verbs, see Appendix B.

Perfect:

נִשְׁמַרְתִּי	נִשְׁמַרְנוּ
נִשְׁמַרְתָּ	נִשְׁמַרְתֶּם
נִשְׁמַרְתְּ	נִשְׁמַרְתֶּן
נִשְׁמַר	נִשְׁמְרוּ
נִשְׁמְרָה	

Imperfect:

אֶשָּׁמֵר	נִשָּׁמֵר
תִּשָּׁמֵר	תִּשָּׁמְרוּ
תִּשָּׁמְרִי	תִּשָּׁמַרְנָה
יִשָּׁמֵר	יִשָּׁמְרוּ
תִּשָּׁמֵר	תִּשָּׁמַרְנָה

Participle: נִשְׁמָר   Imperative: הִשָּׁמֵר

               נִשְׁמֶרֶת   הִשָּׁמְרִי

               נִשְׁמָרִים   הִשָּׁמְרוּ

               נִשְׁמָרוֹת   הִשָּׁמַרְנָה

Cohortatives: נִשָּׁמְרָה ,אִשָּׁמְרָה

Infinitive <u>A</u>:   הִשָּׁמֵר/נִשְׁמֹר

Infinitive <u>C</u>:   [לְ]הִשָּׁמֵר

READING GENESIS 24:41-47

אָז   "then."

אָלָתִי   "my oath." That is, the oath which I made you take. Cf. אָלָה, "an oath." The same word also means a curse.

יִתְּנוּ   Qal imperfect from נתן.

וְהָיִיתָ   "Then you will be." Root: היה.

נָקִי   "free," i.e., released, no longer obligated.

וָאָבֹא   "Accordingly, I came." Qal imperfect of בוֹא.

מַצְלִיחַ   "[You are] prospering." Hiphil participle form from צלח.

הָעַלְמָה   "the young lady."

יֹצֵאת   This form has contracted from יֹצֵאת.

הֹכִיחַ   "[Yahweh] has decided/chosen." Root: יכח.

אֲכַלֶּה   "[before] I could finish." Piel imperfect form of כלה.

לִבִּי   "my heart." Cf. לֵב, לֵבָב, a heart.

וָאֵשְׁתְּ   "So I drank." A Qal imperfect form, shortened because of the Vav-Consecutive. Root: שתה.

הִשְׁקָתָה   "she watered." A Hiphil perfect form from שקה.

וָאָשִׂם   "Then I placed." Qal imperfect of שִׂים.

LESSON 23: THE HIPHIL/HOPHAL CONJUGATIONS

THE FUNCTION OF THE HIPHIL/HOPHAL

The Hiphil stem functions primarily as the causative of the Qal, the Hophal is the passive of the Hiphil. The following chart illustrates the relationship of the Hiphil and Hophal stems to the Qal; other uses will be noted whenever they occur in reading assignments.

Qal	מָלַךְ	"he was king"
Hiph	הִמְלִיךְ	"he made [someone] king"
Hoph	הָמְלַךְ	"he was made king"
Qal	בָּא	"he came"
Hiph	הֵבִיא	"he brought"
Hoph	הוּבָא	"he was brought"
Qal	מֵת	"he died"
Hiph	הֵמִית	"he killed," i.e., caused to die
Hoph	הוּמַת	"he was killed

THE FORM OF THE HIPHIL/HOPHAL

The prepositive letter ה is the characteristic of the Hiphil/Hophal conjugations. The vowels used with ה

will vary in accordance with some of the principles which you have studied earlier (peculiarities of the laryngaels, etc.).

2. The preformative ה appears in the perfect, the imperative, and the infinitive forms.

3. The preformative ה is elided following the preformative letters which are required by forms of the imperfect and the participle.

4. The Hophal initial vowel may be Qibbuṣ, but it is more frequently Qameṣ Hatuph.

Hiphil Perfect: he threw

הִשְׁלַכְתִּי	הִשְׁלַכְנוּ
הִשְׁלַכְתָּ	הִשְׁלַכְתֶּם
הִשְׁלַכְתְּ	הִשְׁלַכְתֶּן
הִשְׁלִיךְ	הִשְׁלִיכוּ
הִשְׁלִיכָה	

Hophal Perfect: he was thrown

הָשְׁלַכְתִּי	הָשְׁלַכְנוּ
הָשְׁלַכְתָּ	הָשְׁלַכְתֶּם
הָשְׁלַכְתְּ	הָשְׁלַכְתֶּן
הָשְׁלַךְ	הָשְׁלְכוּ
הָשְׁלְכָה	

Hiphil Imperfect:

אַשְׁלִיךְ*	נַשְׁלִיךְ
תַּשְׁלִיךְ	תַּשְׁלִיכוּ
תַּשְׁלִיכִי	תַּשְׁלֵכְנָה
יַשְׁלִיךְ	יַשְׁלִיכוּ
תַּשְׁלִיךְ	תַּשְׁלֵכְנָה

*Contracted from אֲהַשְׁלִיךְ, etc.

115

Hophal Imperfect:	אָשְׁלַךְ	נָשְׁלַךְ
	תָּשְׁלַךְ	תָּשְׁלְכוּ
	תָּשְׁלְכִי	תָּשְׁלַכְנָה
	יָשְׁלַךְ	יָשְׁלְכוּ
	תָּשְׁלַךְ	תָּשְׁלַכְנָה

Participles:	מֻשְׁלִךְ	מָשְׁלָךְ
	מֻשְׁלֶכֶת	מָשְׁלֶכֶת
	מֻשְׁלִיכִים	מָשְׁלָכִים
	מֻשְׁלִיכוֹת	מָשְׁלָכוֹת

Imperatives:	הַשְׁלֵךְ	Does not occur.
	הַשְׁלִיכִי	
	הַשְׁלִיכוּ	
	הַשְׁלֵכְנָה	

Cohortatives:	נַשְׁלִיכָה ,אַשְׁלִיכָה
	נַשְׁלְכָה ,אַשְׁלְכָה

Infinitive A: הָשְׁלַךְ ,הַשְׁלֵךְ

Infinitive C: [לְ]הָשְׁלַךְ ,[לְ]הַשְׁלִיךְ

READING GENESIS 24:48-54

וָאֶקֹּד	"So I bowed my head." Root: קדד.
וָאֶשְׁתַּחֲוֶה	"and I prostrated myself."
וָאֲבָרֵךְ	"and I blessed."
הִנְחַנִי	Cf. נחה, "to lead, guide."
לָקַחַת	Qal infinitive construct of לקח.

אִם־יֶשְׁכֶם   " If you (m. pl.) are."

אֵת   "with."

הַגִּידָה   "Tell!" The d.f. in the ג signifies the loss of the first root letter, נ. You should now be able to identify the form.

אֶפְנֶה   Qal Imperfect form of פנה, to turn.

יָמִין   "right [hand]."

אוֹ   "or."

שְׂמֹאל   "left [hand]."

וַיַּעַן   Qal imperfect from עָנָה, "he answered."

נוּכַל   Qal imperfect from יָכֹל, "he was able."

רַע   "bad."

קַח   Qal Imperative, 2 masculine singular of לקח.

לֵךְ   Qal Imperative, 2 masculine singular of הלך.

כְּלִי   "vessels." Cf. כְּלִי, Plural: כֵּלִים, a vessel, a tool, utensil.

מִגְדָנוֹת   "precious things." Lexical form: מִגְדָּנָה.

יִשְׁתּוּ   Qal imperfect of שׁתה.

יֹאכְלוּ   Qal imperfect of אכל.

יָלִינוּ   Qal imperfect of לִין.

יָקוּמוּ   Qal imperfect of קוּם, "to (a)rise."

שַׁלְּחֻנִי   Piel imperative, 3 masculine plural form of שׁלח, "he sent." Note the suffix, "me."

LESSON 24: THE PIEL/PUAL CONJUGATIONS

THE FUNCTION OF THE PIEL/PUAL

The Piel conjugation commonly functions as the intensive of the Qal stem, the Pual is the passive of the Piel. The following chart illustrates the relationship of the Piel and Pual stems to the Qal.

Qal:	שָׁבַר	he broke
Piel:	שִׁבֵּר	he shattered
Pual:	שֻׁבַּר	he was shattered

Verbs which are stative in the Qal may become active of causative in the Piel stem.

Qal:	מָלֵא	he was full
Piel:	מִלֵּא כַּד	he filled a jar
Pual:	מֻלָּא כַּד	a jar was filled

Other functions of the Piel/Pual will be noted whenever they occur in reading assignments.

THE FORM OF THE PIEL/PUAL

1. The morphological characteristic of the Piel/Pual conjugations is the doubling of the second root consonant, a doubling indicated by d.f. If the second root letter is

either a laryngael or a ר it will reject the doubling. The
resultant vowel changes will be noted and explained as they
occur.

     2. The preformative letter pointed with simple or
compound Sheva is a characteristic sign of the Piel/Pual in
its forms of the Imperfect, Participle, and Cohortative.

     3. For basic Piel/Pual forms of irregular verbs,
see Appendix D.

Piel Perfect:	שִׁבַּרְתִּי	שִׁבַּרְנוּ
	שִׁבַּרְתָּ	שִׁבַּרְתֶּם
	שִׁבַּרְתְּ	שִׁבַּרְתֶּן
	שִׁבֵּר	שִׁבְּרוּ
	שִׁבְּרָה	

Pual Perfect:	שֻׁבַּרְתִּי	שֻׁבַּרְנוּ
	שֻׁבַּרְתָּ	שֻׁבַּרְתֶּם
	שֻׁבַּרְתְּ	שֻׁבַּרְתֶּן
	שֻׁבַּר	שֻׁבְּרוּ
	שֻׁבְּרָה	

Piel Imperfect:	אֲשַׁבֵּר	נְשַׁבֵּר
	תְּשַׁבֵּר	תְּשַׁבְּרוּ
	תְּשַׁבְּרִי	תְּשַׁבֵּרְנָה
	יְשַׁבֵּר	יְשַׁבְּרוּ
	תְּשַׁבֵּר	תְּשַׁבֵּרְנָה

Pual Imperfect:	אֲשֻׁכַּר	נְשֻׁכַּר
	תְּשֻׁכַּר	תְּשֻׁכְּרוּ
	תְּשֻׁכְּרִי	תְּשֻׁכַּרְנָה
	יְשֻׁכַּר	יְשֻׁכְּרוּ
	תְּשֻׁכַּר	תְּשֻׁכַּרְנָה

Participles:	מְשֻׁכָּר	מְשֻׁכָּר
	מְשֻׁכֶּרֶת	מְשֻׁכֶּרֶת
	מְשֻׁכָּרִים	מְשֻׁכָּרִים
	מְשֻׁכָּרוֹת	מְשֻׁכָּרוֹת
Imperatives:	שֻׁכַּר	שֻׁכַּר
	שֻׁכְּרִי	שֻׁכְּרִי
	שֻׁכְּרוּ	שֻׁכְּרוּ
	שֻׁכַּרְנָה	שֻׁכַּרְנָה
Cohortatives:	אֲשַׁכְּרָה, נְשַׁכְּרָה	
	אֲשֻׁכְּרָה, נְשֻׁכְּרָה	
Infinitive A:	שֻׁכַּר, שֻׁכֹּר	
Infinitive C:	[לְ]שֻׁכַּר [לְ]שֻׁכֹּר	

READING GENESIS 24:55-61

תשב   Qal jussive form of ישב.

ימים או   "about ten days."
עשור

תלך   Qal imperfect form of הלך.

אתי   "me." See the Note below.

אלכה   Qal imperfect form of הלך.

התלכי   הֲ is the Hebrew question mark. תלכי is a Qal imperfect form of הלך.

אלך   Qal imperfect form of הלך.

מנקתה   Lexical form: מֵינֶ֫קֶת, "a nurse."

היי   Qal jussive, 2 feminine singular form of היה.

אלפי   Cf. אֶ֫לֶף, "one-thousand."

רבבה   "ten-thousand, myriads."

יירש   A contraction from יִירַשׁ, lexical form יָרַשׁ, he possessed, inherited.

זרעך   Lexical form זֶ֫רַע, "a seed, descendant."

שער   "gate."

שנאיו   Cf. שָׂנֵא, "he hated."

ותקם   Qal imperfect form of קוּם.

תרכבנה   In the Qal, רכב means "to ride." In the Piel, it means to mount.

תלכנה   Qal imperfect form of הלך.

יקח   Qal imperfect form of לקח.

ילך   Qal imperfect form of הלך.

NOTE

אֵת often indicates a pronominal direct object by suffixes added directly to it. Note the chart below:

אֹתָ֫נוּ	אֹתִי
אֶתְכֶם	אֹתְךָ
אֶתְכֶן	אֹתָךְ
אֹתָם	אֹתוֹ
אֹתָן	אֹתָהּ

LESSON 25: THE HITPAEL CONJUGATION

THE FUNCTION OF THE HITPAEL

The Hitpael conjugation may function in three very distinct ways:

1. It is often the reflexive of the Qal: הִתְאַפֵּק, "he restrained himself."

2. It may include the idea of "acting as" or of "playing the part": הִתְנַכֵּר, "he acted like a stranger."

3. It may have a reciprocal sense: הִתְרָאוּ, "they stared at each other."

THE FORM OF THE HITPAEL

1. The two characteristics of the Hitpael form are (a) the doubling of the second root consonant [cf. Piel/Pual] and (b) the prefix הִתְ [with ה elided after preformatives].

2. For Hitpael forms of irregular verbs, see Appendix E.

Perfect:

הִתְאַפַּקְתִּי	הִתְאַפַּקְנוּ
הִתְאַפַּקְתָּ	הִתְאַפַּקְתֶּם
הִתְאַפַּקְתְּ	הִתְאַפַּקְתֶּן
הִתְאַפֵּק	הִתְאַפְּקוּ
הִתְאַפְּקָה	

122

Imperfect:

נִתְאַפֵּק	אֶתְאַפֵּק
תִּתְאַפְּקוּ	תִּתְאַפֵּק
תִּתְאַפֵּקְנָה[1]	תִּתְאַפְּקִי
יִתְאַפְּקוּ	יִתְאַפֵּק
תִּתְאַפֵּקְנָה	תִּתְאַפֵּק

Participle:	מִתְאַפֵּק	Imperative:	הִתְאַפֵּק
	מִתְאַפֶּקֶת		הִתְאַפְּקִי
	מִתְאַפְּקִים		הִתְאַפְּקוּ
	מִתְאַפְּקוֹת		הִתְאַפֵּקְנָה

Cohortative: נִתְאַפְּקָה, אֶתְאַפְּקָה

Infinitive A: הִתְאַפֵּק

Infinitive C: [לְ]הִתְאַפֵּק

SPECIAL NOTE

When the first root letter of a verb is either a fricative [שׁ שׂ ס ז] or an affricate [צ], it exchanges places with the ת. Thus,

שָׁמַר becomes הִשְׁתַּמֵּר.

After metathesis with צ, ת becomes ט. Thus, צָדֵק

becomes הִצְטַדֵּק.

---

[1]The second and third persons feminine plural may also be written תִּתְאַפֵּקְנָה.

READING GENESIS 24:62-67

בָּא   "had come."   Root: בּוֹא.

מִבּוֹא   "from going."

יֵצֵא   Qal imperfect form of יָצָא.

לָשׂוּחַ   "to meditate."

לִפְנוֹת   "toward, at the beginning of, before."

יִשָּׂא   Qal imperfect form of נָשָׂא, he raised, lifted.

יַרְא   Qal imperfect form of רָאָה.

בָּאִים   "[camels] were coming."

תִּפֹּל   Qal imperfect form of נפל, he fell.

הַלָּזֶה   An older spelling of הַזֶּה.

צָעִיף   "veil."

תִּתְכָּס   Root: כסה, he covered.

יְסַפֵּר   The Piel of ספר means to tell, recount.

יְבִאֶהָ   Hiphil imperfect form of בּוֹא.

הָאֹהֱלָה   Lexical form: אֹהֶל, a tent.

יִנָּחֵם   "[Isaac] was comforted."   Form _____?

SPECIAL NOTE

In this lesson and earlier you have observed that the Hebrew verb often takes a pronominal suffix. Refer to the chart "Pronominal Suffixes With The Verb", pp. 220-221.

Vocabulary Review Lessons 21 - 25

These words should be learned before going on to Lesson 26.

רָעֵב	עַלְמָה
שָׂכָל	יֹצֵאת
שָׁכֵן	יָכֹז
זָקֵן	לֵב, לֵבָב
קָטֹן	יָמִין
צָמֵא	אוֹ
שָׁכַב, שְׁכַב	שְׂמֹאל
גָּדַל	יָכֹל
כָּבֵד	פְּלִי
קָדַד	מִגְדָּנָה
אָדוֹן	שָׁלַח
עָזַב	מֵינֶקֶת
אֱמֶת	אֶלֶף
נָחָה	רְבָבָה
פֹּה	זֶרַע
פָּנָה	רָכַב
פָּתָה	שִׁיהַ
רָחַץ	הַזֶּה
שִׁפְחָה	צָעִיף
מִשְׁפָּחָה	פָּסָה
צָלָה	סֵפֶר
אָז	אֹהֶל
אֵלָה	נָחָם
נָקִי	

THE STRONG VERB

Because of a convention which developed in Hebrew grammar books as early as medieval times, some rather uncommon terminology is used to describe the various patterns of inflection which the Hebrew verb can exhibit. Using the three root consonants פעל, "work", as a pattern, Hebrew grammarians began the practice of naming all verbs similarly. The first letter of a root was termed the פ letter, the second the ע letter, and the third the ל letter. Thus,

אכל is a Pe-Aleph verb;

כלה is a Lamed-He verb;

נטה is a Pe-Nun/Lamed-He verb; etc.

The word פעל also came to be used as a pattern for other verbs when discussions of derived stems took place. For example, since the passive of פָּעַל was נִפְעַל, grammarians began to speak of the Qal passive form of any verb as its "nif'al". Thus the passive of כָּמַר, which is spelled נִכְמַר, was termed the "nif al" of כמר.

The complete list of verbal terms derived from the pattern of inflections which פעל takes, may be charted as follows[1]:

---

[1]Learn these terms well, for they will be used to describe verb forms from now on.

	קל פעל (Pa'al) Qal	נִפְעַל Niphal	פִּעֵל Piel	פֻּעַל Pual	הִפְעִיל Hiphil	הָפְעַל Hophal	הִתְפַּעֵל Hithpael
Prf. 3	שָׁמַר	נִשְׁמַר	שִׁמֵּר	שֻׁמַּר	הִשְׁמִיר	הָשְׁמַר	הִשְׁתַּמֵּר
Imprf.	יִשְׁמֹר	יִשָּׁמֵר	יְשַׁמֵּר	יְשֻׁמַּר	יַשְׁמִיר	יָשְׁמַר	יִשְׁתַּמֵּר
Imv.	שְׁמֹר	הִשָּׁמֵר	שַׁמֵּר	—	הַשְׁמֵר	(הָשְׁמַר)	הִשְׁתַּמֵּר
Inf. C.	שְׁמֹר	הִשָּׁמֵר	שַׁמֵּר	שֻׁמַּר	הַשְׁמִיר	הָשְׁמַר	הִשְׁתַּמֵּר
Inf. A.	שָׁמוֹר	נִשְׁמֹר	שַׁמֵּר	—	הַשְׁמֵר	הָשְׁמֵר	הִשְׁתַּמֵּר
Ptc.	שׁוֹמֵר	נִשְׁמָר	מְשַׁמֵּר	מְשֻׁמָּר	מַשְׁמִיר	מָשְׁמָר	מִשְׁתַּמֵּר

Notes:

1. Terms for derived stems are transliterations of Hebrew terms derived from פעל.

2. Perfect and Imperfect forms are 3rd masculine singular; Imperative forms are 2nd masculine singular.

3. Notice the relationship between Imperfect, Imperative, and Infinitive Construct.

4. Notice participles with מ preformative.

5. Qal, simple active; Niphal, simple passive; Piel, intensive active; Pual, intensive passive; Hiphil, causative active; Hophal, causative passive; Hithpael, intensive or reflexive.

6. In the Hithpael metathesis of שׁ and ת.

NOTE:

A chart with all possible different forms of the strong verb is included in the appendix, page 222.

LESSON 26: PE-NUN VERB

As you have already seen, the so-called "regular" verb is relatively rare in Hebrew. A "regular" verb is one with three consonants, none of which is weak in any way -- a laryngael, etc. In this and the next few chapters you will study several classes of "irregular" verbs. The first of these classes is the Pe-Nun Verb.

Most Pe-Nun verbs are regular in the Qal Perfect and in the Qal active Participle forms. However, following a preformative letter, such as occurs in the Qal Imperfect, the initial NUN is assimilated. Observe the conjugation of נָגַשׁ, "he drew near". It is not used in the Qal Perfect; it is a normal conjugation in the Piel/Pual stem and in the Hitpael.

QAL

Imperative: גַּשׁ

גְּשִׁי

גְּשׁוּ

גַּשְׁנָה

Infinitive A: נָגוֹשׁ

Infinitive C: [לְ] גֶּשֶׁת

Imperfect: אֶגַּשׁ

תִּגַּשׁ

תִּגְּשִׁי

יִגַּשׁ

תִּגַּשׁ

נִגַּשׁ

תִּגְּשׁוּ

תִּגַּשְׁנָה

יִגְּשׁוּ

128

NIPHAL

Perfect: נִגַּעְתָּ, נִגַּעְתִּי, etc.

Imperfect: תִּנָּגַע, אֶנָּגַע, etc.

Participle: נִגָּעוֹת, נִגָּעִים, נִגַּעַת, נִגָּע

Imperative: הִנָּגַע, הִנָּגְעִי, הִנָּגְעוּ, הִנָּגַעְנָה

Cohortative: נִנָּגְעָה, אֶנָּגְעָה

Infinitive A: הִנָּגֵעַ

Infinitive C: [לְ]הִנָּגַע

HIPHIL

Perfect:		Imperfect:	
הִגַּעְתִּי		אַגִּיעַ	
הִגַּעְתָּ		תַּגִּיעַ	
הִגַּעְתְּ		תַּגִּיעִי	
הִגִּיעַ		יַגִּיעַ	
הִגִּיעָה		תַּגִּיעַ	
הִגַּעְנוּ		נַגִּיעַ	
הִגַּעְתֶּם		תַּגִּיעָה	
הִגַּעְתֶּן		תַּגַּעְנָה	
הִגִּיעוּ		יַגִּיעוּ	

Participle: מַגִּיעַ, מַגַּעַת, מַגִּיעִים, מַגִּיעוֹת

Imperative: הַגַּע, הַגִּיעִי, הַגִּיעָה, הַגַּעְנָה

Infinitive A: הַגֵּעַ

Infinitive C: [לְ]הַגִּיעַ

NOTES

1. The נ is regularly assimilated following the preformative letters. That assimilation is signaled in the next letter by the Daghesh Forte.

2. The נ of most Pe-Nun verbs drops entirely in the formation of the imperative and the infinitive construct.

3. One important exception to note two above is the word נפל, "he fell". It has the form נְפֹל for its imperative and its infinitive construct. This is due to the presence of an "o" sounding thematic vowel. נפל also forms its Qal Imperfect with the "o" class vowel. Thus,

$$\text{אֶפֹּל} \quad \text{תִּפֹּל} \quad \text{יִפֹּל} \quad \text{נִפֹּל} \quad \text{תִּפְּלָה} \quad \text{תִּפֹּלְנָה}$$

נתן

נתן, "he gave", while classified as Pe-Nun, presents added inflectional variations because it is also Lamed-Nun. Accordingly, it conjugates as follows in the Qal:

Perfect:		Imperfect:	
נָתַֽתִּי		אֶתֵּן	
נָתַֽתָּ		תִּתֵּן	
נָתַֽתְּ		תִּתְּנִי	
נָתַן		יִתֵּן	
נָתְנָה		תִּתֵּן	
נָתַֽנּוּ		נִתֵּן	
נְתַתֶּם		תִּתְּנוּ	
נְתַתֶּן		תִּתֵּֽנָּה	
נָתְנוּ		יִתְּנוּ	

Imperative: תֵּֽנָה ,תְּנוּ ,תְּנִי ,תֵּן

Infinitive A: נָתוֹן

Infinitive C: נְתֵת[לָ]

NOTES

1. In the Infinitive Construct, תֵּת is written for the expected form תְּנְתּ.

2. נתן is regular in the Qal Participle.

3. The final Nun is dropped in places where it would receive Silent Sheva and thus would remain essentially vowelless.

4. The Ṣere should be observed in each place where it occurs.

לקח

The ל in לקח is treated as if it were a Nun. Its conjugation is regular in the Qal Perfect, the Qal Active Participle, and the entire Niphal and Hitpael conjugations. It does not occur in the Piel/Pual or the Hiphil/Hophal conjugations. Note its unusual Qal forms in the lists below.

Imperative: קַח

קְחִי

קְחוּ

קַ֫חְנָה

Infinitive A: לָקוֹחַ

Infinitive C: [לְ]קַ֫חַת

Imperfect: אֶקַּח

תִּקַּח

תִּקְחִי

יִקַּח

תִּקַּח

נִקַּח

תִּקְחוּ

תִּקַּ֫חְנָה

יִקְחוּ

131

EXERCISE

Below are several Pe-Nun verbs which you have seen
in a reading passage from Genesis. Be prepared to translate
and identify each word.

קַח וַיִּקַּח וַיִּשָּׂא לֹא תִקַּח וְלָקַחְתָּ לְקָחַנִי אֶתֵּן וַיִּתֵּן יִתְּנָה לָקַחַת

נָתַן וַתִּשָּׂא וַתִּפֹּל וַתִּקַּח נָפַל

READING GENESIS 25:1-6

ויסף "and [Abraham] added/increased." This is a Hiphil
imperfect form of יסף, a verb which is often [as
here] used adverbially to mean "again". Thus the
entire phrase, ויסף אברהם ויקח אשה, simply means:
"Then Abraham took a wife again," or "Abraham took
another wife."

ותלד "and she bore." Qal imperfect of ילד.

היו Qal imperfect, third common plural of היה.

פילגשים Cf. פילגש, "a concubine".

מתנת Cf. מתנה, "a gift".

מעל "away from". Literally, "from upon" or "from
near". This is a compound preposition, mixing
together מן and על.

בעודנו חי "while he was still living". בעוד is a combination
of ב and עוד, "yet, or still". To it a third person
masculine singular suffix has been added. The
suffix functions as the subject of the phrase and
the verb of the phrase is חי, a masculine singular
form of the adjective "living", which derives from
the root היה, "he is alive".

132

LESSON 27: THE PE-VAV AND PE-YOD VERBS

There are two kinds of Hebrew verbs which begin with the letter Yod.

1. Verbs which may be classified as originally Pe-Yod.

2. Verbs whose lexical form in biblical Hebrew appears as Pe-Yod but whose original first letter was Vav. Such (originally Pe-Vav) Pe-Yod verbs exhibit certain peculiarities which the paradigms and the notes below will explain. For the paradigms, three words have been chosen which you have already seen in some form: יָשַׁב: sit, dwell; יָדַע: know; and יָלַד: bear (children). Their Qal Perfect forms correspond closely to שָׁמַר. Their Qal Imperfect, Imperative, and Infinitive Construct forms show the loss of the Yod which was originally Vav.

Imperfect:		
אֵשֵׁב	אֵדַע	אֵלֵד
תֵּשֵׁב	תֵּדַע	תֵּלֵד
תֵּשְׁבִי	תֵּדְעִי	תֵּלְדִי
יֵשֵׁב	יֵדַע	יֵלֵד
תֵּשֵׁב	תֵּדַע	תֵּלֵד
נֵשֵׁב	נֵדַע	נֵלֵד
תֵּשְׁבוּ	תֵּדְעוּ	תֵּלְדוּ
תֵּשַׁבְנָה	תֵּדַעְנָה	תֵּלַדְנָה
יֵשְׁבוּ	יֵדְעוּ	יֵלְדוּ

Imperative:	שֵׁב	דַּע	לֵד
	שְׁבִי	דְּעִי	לְדִי
	שְׁבוּ	דְּעוּ	לְדוּ
	שֵׁבְנָה	דַּעְנָה	לֵדְנָה
Infinitive C:	[לָ]שֶׁבֶת	[לָ]דַּעַת	[לָ]לֶדֶת

NOTES

    1. These verbs build their imperfect and imperative forms on a biconsonantal base which employs only the last two root letters. The vowel used is regularly Ṣere.

    2. The preformative letters for the imperfect are also regularly vocalized with Ṣere.

    3. The laryngael in ידע causes the change from a Ṣere to a Pataḥ.

    4. To form the infinitive construct, these words simply add ת to the biconsonantal base.

הלך

    הלך is a frequently-used word which conjugates like an original Pe-Vav verb. Its conjugation is regular in the Qal Perfect, but takes the following forms in the imperfect, imperative, and infinitive construct:

Imperfect:	אֵלֵךְ	נֵלֵךְ
	תֵּלֵךְ	תֵּלְכוּ
	תֵּלְכִי	תֵּלַכְנָה
	יֵלֵךְ	יֵלְכוּ
	תֵּלֵךְ	

Imperative:	לֵךְ	Infinitive C:	[לָ]לֶכֶת
	לְכִי		
	לְכוּ		
	לֵכְנָה		

HIPHIL[1]

Pe-Vav/Yod verbs exhibit special characteristics in the Hiphil conjugation which necessitates the re-appearance of the original Vav. The Hiphil forms of ילד illustrate:

Perfect:	הוֹלַדְתִּי	Imperfect:	אוֹלִיד
	הוֹלַדְתָּ		תּוֹלִיד
	הוֹלַדְתְּ		תּוֹלִידִי
	הוֹלִיד		יוֹלִיד
	הוֹלִידָה		תּוֹלִיד
	הוֹלַדְנוּ		נוֹלִיד
	הוֹלַדְתֶּם		תּוֹלִידוּ
	הוֹלַדְתֶּן		תּוֹלֵדְנָה
	הוֹלִידוּ		יוֹלִידוּ
Participle:	מוֹלִיד	Imperative:	הוֹלֵד
	מוֹלִידָה		הוֹלִידִי
	מוֹלִידִים		הוֹלִידוּ
	מוֹלִידוֹת		הוֹלֵדְנָה
Infinitive Construct:	[לְ]הוֹלִיד		

---

[1]To obtain the Hophal forms, change Ḥolem to Shureq and use Pataḥ as the thematic vowel.

NIPHAL

ידע is also a good example of the Niphal forms of Pe-Vav/Yod verbs.

Perfect: נוֹלַדְתִּי   Imperfect: אִוָּלֵד

נוֹלַדְתָּ   תִּוָּלֵד

נוֹלַדְתְּ   תִּוָּלְדִי

נוֹלַד   יִוָּלֵד

נוֹלְדָה   תִּוָּלֵד

נוֹלַדְנוּ   נִוָּלֵד

נוֹלַדְתֶּם   תִּוָּלְדוּ

נוֹלַדְתֶּן   תִּוָּלַדְנָה

נוֹלְדוּ   יִוָּלְדוּ

Participle: נוֹלָד   Imperative: הִוָּלֵד

נוֹלֶדֶת   הִוָּלְדִי

נוֹלָדִים   הִוָּלְדוּ

נוֹלָדוֹת   הִוָּלַדְנָה

Infinitive Construct: [לְ]הִוָּלֵד

PIEL/PUAL

Pe-Vav/Yod verbs are regular throughout the Piel and Pual conjugations.

HITPAEL

In the Hitpael, many Pe-Vav/Yod verbs are regular:

הֹתילד, etc. Others may be patterned after ידע (see Appendix E).

STATIVE VERBS יכל AND ירא

ירא exhibits characteristic variations for Stative Pe-Vav/Yod verbs in its Imperfect and related forms:

Qal Imperfect: <u></u> תִּירָא, אִירָא, etc.

Qal Imperative: <u></u> יְרָאנָה, יְראוּ, יִרְאִי, יְרָא

Qal Infinitive Construct: <u></u> [לְ]יִרֹא

יכל exhibits anomalous Imperfect forms which should be memorized.

אוּכַל	נוּכַל
תּוּכַל	תּוּכְלוּ
תּוּכְלִי	תּוּכַלְנָה
יוּכַל	יוּכְלוּ
תּוּכַל	

ORIGINAL PE-YOD

There are only a few verbs which are true, original Pe-Yod types. They inflect in the same way the statives do (see above). Cf. יטב, be good, pleasing:

Qal Imperfect: <u></u> יִיטַב

Hiphil Perfect: <u></u> הֵיטִיב

Hiphil Imperfect: <u></u> יֵיטִיב

Hiphil Participle: <u></u> מֵיטִיב

EXERCISE

As a review, identify and translate the following Pe-Vav/Yod verbs. All of them are forms which you have already read in Genesis.

יֶלֶד   יָ֫לַד   וַיֵּ֫שֶׁב   וְיִרַשׁ   וְיָדַ֫עְתִּי   נֵלְכָה   וַיֵּלְכוּ   וַיֵּ֫לֶךְ   וְלֵהֹ־לֵךְ

וַתֵּ֫רֶד   יָדְעָה   אֵדַע   צֵאת   יֵצֵאת   לָלֶ֫כֶת   תֵּלֵךְ   יוֹשֵׁב   וַתֵּ֫לֶד

אֵלֶּה   תֵּלֵךְ   הֹשֵׁב   וַיּוֹצֵא   וְלֵךְ   נוּכַל   יָצָא   הַיֹּצֵאת   לָדַ֫עַת

VOCABULARY FOR GENESIS 25:7-15

חַיִּים	life	בְּכֹר	first-born (son)
שֶׁ֫בַע	seven (f.)	שִׁבְעִים	seventy
חָמֵשׁ	five (f.)	גָּוַע	he expired, died
אָסַף	he gathered	תּוֹלְדָה	a generation; always in the plural: תּוֹלְדוֹת
מָ֫וֶת	death; construct state: מוֹת		
		שֵׂיב, שֵׂיבָה	gray hairs, old age, maturity
שָׂבַע	he was satisfied, full		

LESSON 28: THE HOLLOW VERBS

Morphologically, there are two important points which should be remembered about Hollow verbs.

1. First, hollow verbs are derived from biconsonantal or two-lettered roots. Thus, in the word בוא, the medial ו is a long vowel, not one of the root consonants.

2. Second, because the ו is not the middle root letter, the lexical form of בוא (and all hollow verbs) is not the third person masculine singular perfect of the Qal but rather the Qal infinitive construct.

Four of the most common hollow verbs are conjugated below. Study carefully the forms of each, for all four of the words occur hundreds of times in the Hebrew Bible.

בוֹא   to come

מוּת   to die

שִׂים   to put, place

שׁוּב   to return, turn

QAL PERFECT

שַׁבְתִּי	שַׂמְתִּי	מַתִּי	בָּאתִי
שַׁבְתָּ	שַׂמְתָּ	מַתָּ	בָּאתָ
שַׁבְתְּ	שַׂמְתְּ	מַתְּ	בָּאת
שָׁב	שָׂם	מֵת	בָּא
שָׁבָה	שָׂמָה	מֵתָה	בָּאָה
שַׁבְנוּ	שַׂמְנוּ	מַתְנוּ	בָּאנוּ
שַׁבְתֶּם	שַׂמְתֶּם	מַתֶּם	בָּאתֶם
שַׁבְתֶּן	שַׂמְתֶּן	מַתֶּן	בָּאתֶן
שָׁבוּ	שָׂמוּ	מֵתוּ	בָּאוּ

QAL IMPERFECT

אָשׁוּב	אָשִׂים	אָמוּת	אָבוֹא
תָּשׁוּב	תָּשִׂים	תָּמוּת	תָּבוֹא
תָּשׁוּבִי	תָּשִׂימִי	תָּמוּתִי	תָּבוֹאִי
יָשׁוּב	יָשִׂים	יָמוּת	יַבוֹת
תָּשׁוּב	תָּשִׂים	תָּמוּת	תָּבוֹא
נָשׁוּב	נָשִׂים	נָמוּת	נָבוֹא
תָּשׁוּבוּ	תָּשִׂימוּ	תָּמוּתוּ	תָּבוֹאוּ
תְּשׁוּבֶינָה	תְּשִׂימֶנָה	תְּמוּתֶינָה	תְּבוֹאֶינָה
תָּשֹׁבְנָה	תָּשֵׂמְנָה	תָּמֹתְנָה	תָּבוֹאנָה
יָשׁוּבוּ	יָשִׂימוּ	יָמוּתוּ	יָבוֹאוּ

QAL PARTICIPLE

שָׁב   שָׂם   מֵת   בָּא

שָׁבָה   שָׂמָה   מֵתָה   בָּאָה

שָׁבִים   שָׂמִים   מֵתִים   בָּאִים

שָׁבוֹת   שָׂמוֹת   מֵתוֹת   בָּאוֹת

QAL IMPERATIVE

שׁוּב   שִׂים   מוּת   בּוֹא

שׁוּבִי   שִׂימִי   מוּתִי   בּוֹאִי

שׁוּבוּ   שִׂימוּ   מוּתוּ   בּוֹאוּ

שֹׁבְנָה   שֵׂמְנָה   מֹתְנָה   בּוֹאנָה

QAL COHORTATIVE

אָשׁוּבָה   אָשִׂימָה   אָמוּתָה   אָבוֹאָה

נָשׁוּבָה   נָשִׂימָה   נָמוּתָה   נָבוֹאָה

INFINITIVE ABSOLUTE

שׁוֹב   שׂוֹם   מוֹת   בּוֹא

INFINITIVE CONSTRUCT

[לָ]שׁוּב   [לָ]שִׂים   [לָ]מוּת   [לָ]בוֹא

1. The hollow verbs exhibit a system of accent different from that used for regular verbs. Study carefully the forms given in the paradigms above and note the position of the accent.

2. In the Imperfect, the bracketed forms are the second and/or third person feminine plural forms; the last form written is the third person masculine plural. It is important to remember that both of the forms listed sometimes occur. There is no set rule describing when one or the other form will appear.

3. The imperfect with the Vav-Consecutive presents a special case. Because the accent is pulled toward the ו, the second Qameṣ of the form must be a Ḥaṭuph. Cf.

וַיָּקָם   va-yáqom

וַיָּרָץ   va-yároṣ

וַתָּרָץ   va-tároṣ

וַיֵּשֶׁב   va-yéšov

4. For basic forms of the derived conjugations, see Lessons 34, 35, 36, and 37. These list both Hollow Verbs and other irregular verbal types.

VOCABULARY FOR GENESIS 25:16-21

חָצֵר	a village	בָּנָה	he built
טִירָה	a camp, encampment	כָּלָה	he finished, ceased
נָשִׂיא	a prince, chief	נָטָה	he extended, stretched
אֻמָּה	a family, tribe	עָנָה	he answered, replied
אַרְבַּע	four (f.)	רָבָה	he multiplied, became great, numerous
אַרְבָּעִים	forty	שָׁתָה	he drank
עָתַר	he entreated	בכה	Qal: he wept; Hiph: he looked sad

לְנֹכַח	in behalf of	פָּנָה	he turned (towards)
עָקָר	adj. sterile, barren	רָעָה	he fed, tended
הָרָה	[to] conceive, become pregant	שׁחה	he bowed down
עָלָה	he went up	נָקָה	he was innocent, clear
עָשָׂה	Qal: he made Piel: he forced, pressed	שׁקה	he let drink, gave to drink, watered
רָאָה	he saw		

LESSON 29: THE GEMINATE VERBS

The Geminate Verb, also called Double 'Ayin Verb, is a verb with the same consonant for the second and third letter of the root or stem.

Regular Geminate Verbs are not difficult to understand if the following points are remembered:

1. The third consonant is a repetition or lengthening of the second in an attempt to conform to the normal triliteral pattern of the verb.

2. This third consonant does not always appear in a form, particularly those forms of the derived conjugations.

3. If there are three letters in a form [סֹבֵב, סָבְבָה] they constitute the root letters which you need to know for using a lexicon and finding the meaning of the word.

4. If only two letters appear, the second letter will be doubled [יָסֹבּוּ, נָסַבּוּ] unless it is final [יָסֹב, הָסֵב].

5. The intensive stems are Poel (act.) and Poal (pass.)

QAL STEM

Perfect		Imperfect	
Sing.		**Sing.**	
1st c.	סַבּֿוֹתִי		אָסֹב
2nd m.	סַבּֿוֹתָ		תָּסֹב
2nd f.	סַבּֿוֹת	etc.	תָּסֹֿבִּי
3rd m.	סָבַב	יָסֹב	יָסֹב
3rd f.	סָבְבָה		תָּסֹב
Plural		**Plural**	
1st c.	סַבּֿוֹנוּ		נָסֹב
2nd m.	סַבּֿוֹתֶם		תָּסֹֿבּוּ
2nd f.	סַבּֿוֹתֶן		תְּסֻבֶּֿינָה
3rd m.	סָבְבוּ		יָסֹֿבּוּ
3rd f.			תְּסֻבֶּֿינָה

Imperative		Participle	
Sing.		**Sing.**	
masc.	סֹב		סֹבֵב
Fem.	סֹֿבִּי		סֹבְבָה
Plural		**Plural**	
Masc.	סֹֿבּוּ		סֹבְבִים
Fem.	סֻבֶּֿינָה		סֹבְבוֹת

Infinitive Absolute	Infinitive Construct
סָבוֹב	סֹב

	NIPHAL	HIPHIL	HOPH'AL	PO'EL	PO'AL
Perf. s. 3m.	נָסַב	הֵסֵב	הוּסַב	סוֹבֵב	סוֹבַב
Impf. s. 3m.	יִסַּב	יָסֵב	יוּסַב	יְסוֹבֵב	יְסוֹבַב
Imv. s. 2m.	הִסַּב	הָסֵב		סוֹבֵב	
Inf. Constr.	הִסַּב	הָסֵב		סוֹבֵב	
Inf. Abs.	הִסּוֹב				
Ptc. s. m.	נָסָב	מֵסֵב	מוּסָב	מְסוֹבֵב	מְסוֹבָב

VOCABULARY FOR GENESIS 25:22-26

רִאשׁוֹן	first, former	הִתְרֹצֵץ	he struggled [with]
אַדְמוֹנִי	red-haired, ruddy	דָּרַשׁ	he asked, enquired
אַדֶּר	a cloak	בֶּטֶן	belly, womb
שֵׂעִיר	hairy	מֵעִים	intestines, belly
עָקֵב	a heel	פָּרַד	he separated
שִׁשָּׁה	six; Fem: שֵׁשׁ	לְאֹם	a people, nation
שִׁשִּׁים	sixty	אָמֵץ	he was powerful
נָגַשׁ	he approached	צָעִיר	small, young
נָשָׂא	he lifted up	תָּאַם	it was double
רָצַץ	he bruised, crushed	נגע	Qal: touch, strike Niph: be striken Hiph: reach, arrive
תְּאֹם	a twin		
תְּאוֹמִים	twins		

SPECIAL NOTE

Hebrew does not have a comparative adjective as a separate form. The preposition מִן is used to show comparison, as verse 23 of this reading exercise illustrates.

146

וּלְאֹם מִלְאֹם יֶאֱמָץ should be translated "and [one] people will be stronger than the [other] people." מִן is used here to strengthen the imperfect form יֶאֱמָץ, "[one] will be strong." The meaning is clearly that one people will be(come) more powerful than the other.

Cf. also the phrase עָצַמְתָּ מִמֶּנּוּ מְאֹד, "you are much greater than we are," Genesis 26:16 below.

מִן is also used with adjectival forms:

גָּד גָּדוֹל מִדָּן: Gad is bigger than Dan.

שָׂרָה גְּדוֹלָה מֵרוּת: Sarah is bigger than Ruth.

Vocabulary Review Lessons 26 - 29

These words should be learned before going on to Lesson 30.

דָּרַשׁ

בֶּטֶן

מֵעִים

פֶּרֶד

לְאֹם

אָמֵץ

צָעִיר

תְּאַם

נָגַע

הָרָה

עָלָה

בָּנָה

נָסָה

רָבָה

בָּכָה

פָּנָה

רָעָה

שָׁחָה

נָקָה

שָׁקָה

רִאשׁוֹן

אַדְמוֹנִי

אֶדֶר

שֵׂעִיר

עָקֵב

שִׁשָּׁה

שִׁשִּׁים

נָגַשׁ

נָשָׂא

רָצַץ

תְּאֹם

תְּאוֹמִים

הִתְרֹצֵץ

יָסַף

מַתָּנָה

עוֹד

הַיִט

שֶׂבַע

חֹמֶשׁ

אָסַף

מוֹת

שָׁבַע

שִׁבְעִים

גָּרַע

תּוֹלֵדָה

שֵׂיב

שֵׂיבָה

חָצֵר

טִירָה

נָשִׂיא

אַמָּה

אַרְבַּע

אַרְבָּעִים

עָתַר

לְנֹכַח

עָקָר

חָיָה

THE WEAK VERBS

	Pe-Nun נגש	Pe-Vav ישב	Pe-Yod יטב	Hollow בוא	קום	Ayin-Double סבב
Qal Prf.	נִגַּשׁ	יָשַׁב	יָטַב	בָּא	קָם	סַב סָבַב
Impf.	יִגַּשׁ	יֵשֵׁב	יִיטַב	יָבוֹא	יָקוּם	יָסֹב
Imv.	גַּשׁ	שֵׁב	טַב	בּוֹא	קוּם	סֹב
Inf.	גֶּשֶׁת	שֶׁבֶת	טֶבֶת	בּוֹא	קוּם	סֹב
Ptc.	נֹגֵשׁ	יוֹשֵׁב	(יוֹטֵב)	בָּא	קָם	סוֹבֵב
Piel Prf.	נִגֵּשׁ	יִשֵּׁב	——	——	קוֹמֵם	סוֹבֵב
Impf.	יְנַגֵּשׁ	יְיַשֵּׁב	——	——	יְקוֹמֵם	יְסוֹבֵב
Imv	נַגֵּשׁ	יַשֵּׁב	——	——	קוֹמֵם	סוֹבֵב
Inf.	נַגֵּשׁ	יַשֵּׁב	——	——	קוֹמֵם	סוֹבֵב
Ptc.	מְנַגֵּשׁ	מְיַשֵּׁב	——	——	מְקוֹמֵם	מְסוֹבֵב
Hiph. Prf.	הִגִּישׁ	הוֹשִׁיב	הוֹטִיב	הֵבִיא	הֵקִים	הֵסֵב
Impf.	יַגִּישׁ	יוֹשִׁיב	יוֹטִיב	יָבִיא	יָקִים	יָסֵב יָסֹב
Imv.	הַגֵּשׁ	הוֹשֵׁב	הוֹטֵב	——	הָקֵם	הָסֵב
Inf.	הַגִּישׁ	הוֹשִׁיב	הוֹטִיב	הָבִיא	הָקִים	הָסֵב
Ptc.	מַגִּישׁ	מוֹשִׁיב	מוֹטִיב	מֵבִיא	מֵקִים	מֵסֵב

CHARACTERISTICS OF WEAK VERBS

The characteristics of Weak Verbs listed below are the main <u>differences</u> between the Weak Verbs and the Strong Verbs.

Pe-Nun Verbs

1. Nun assimilated in Qal Imperfect (e.g. יִגַּשׁ), Hiphil Perfect (e.g. הִגִּישׁ) and Imperfect (e.g. יַגִּישׁ), and Hophal Perfect (e.g. הֻגַּשׁ) and Imperfect (e.g. יֻגַּשׁ).

2. The Qal Infinitive Construct is characterized in most instances by the absence of initial Nun and the addition of a Tav as the final letter (e.g. גֶּשֶׁת).

3. The verb לקח is treated like a Pe-Nun verb in the Qal Imperfect (e.g. יִקַּח).

Pe-Yod/Pe-Vav Verbs

1. Original Pe-Vav verbs build their Imperfect and Imperative on a bi-consonantal base of only the last two letters of the root. The vowel of the preformative of Imperfects is regularly Ṣere (e.g. יֵשֵׁב).

2. The Qal Infinitive Construct is formed in most cases in the use of the last two root letters and a final Tav (e.g. שֶׁבֶת).

3. The Qal Imperfects of original Pe-Yod verbs are formed with an î-vowel as the preformative vowel. (e.g. יִירַשׁ).

4. The Niphal retains the original Vav in the Perfect as the preformative vowel (e.g. נוֹלַד), and as a pointed first-root letter in the Imperfect (e.g. יִוָּלֵד), and Imperative (e.g. הִוָּלֵד).

5. The Hiphil retains the Vav as the preformative vowel in the Perfect (e.g. הוֹלִיד) and in the Imperfect (e.g. יוֹלִיד), Imperative (e.g. הוֹלֵד), Infinitive (e.g. הוֹלִיד), and Participle (e.g. מוֹלִיד).

6. The verb הלך is treated as a Pe-Vav verb in the Qal Imperfect (e.g. יֵלֵךְ).

Hollow Verbs

1. The forms of the Qal Perfect are based on two-lettered roots without the middle Vav or Yod (e.g. קָם).

2. The preformative vowel of the Imperfect is regularly Qames (e.g. יָקוּם).

3. The Hiphil is pointed regularly with Ṣere as the preformative vowel of the Perfect (e.g. הֵקִים) and Qames as the preformative vowel of the Imperfect (e.g. יָקִים).

4. The Hophal regularly uses Shureq as the preformative vowel of the perfect (e.g. הוּקַם) and of the imperfect (יוּקַם).

5. The intensive forms employ reduplication of the last letter in both Polel (e.g. קוֹמֵם) and Polal (e.g. קוֹמַם).

Geminate Verbs

1. The Qal Imperfect employs two patterns for the imperfect: 1) with preformative a-vowel (יָסֹב) and 2) with preformative vowel ḥireq with doubling (יִסֹב).

2. The Niphal utilizes the following as preformative vowels: in the perfect the Qames (נָסַב) and in the imperfect the Ḥireq with doubling (יִסַּב).

3. The Hiphil Stem uses the following as preformative vowels: in the perfect the Ṣere (e.g. הֵסֵב) and in the imperfect Qames (e.g. יָסֵב) or the Pathaḥ with doubling (e.g. יַסֵּב).

4. The Hophal Stem uses the following as the preformative vowels: in the perfect the Shureq (e.g. הוּסַב) and in the imperfect the Shureq (e.g. יוּסַב) or Qibbuṣ with doubling (e.g. יֻסַּב).

5. Intensive stems retain the reduplication: Po'el (e.g. סוֹבֵב) and Po'al (e.g. סוֹבַב).

LESSON 30: THE PE-LARYNGAEL VERBS

The laryngaels [ע ח ה א] exhibit three distinct characteristics which set them apart from the other letters of the Hebrew alphabet.

1. They cannot be doubled (lengthened) and thus reject Daghesh Forte.

2. They prefer "a" class vowels, often requiring the Patah under them and even just before them.

3. They are pointed with compound Sheva in places where simple Sheva would stand under another letter.

QAL

In the Qal, only the Imperfect shows inflectional changes which the three rules given above do not explain. For the active verb, Qal Imperfect is normally תַעֲזֹב, אֶעֱזֹב, etc. For the stative verb, the thematic vowel is Patah: תֶחֱרַד, אֶחֱרַד, etc. The Stative Qal Participle inflects as an adjective: חֲרֵדוֹת, חֲרֵדִים, חֲרֵדָה, חָרֵד.

NIPHAL

In the Niphal Imperfect, because the initial letter

cannot be doubled, the preceding vowel must be lengthened compensatorily: אֵעָזֵב, etc. Other Niphal forms are self-explanatory.

HIPHIL

In the Hiphil Imperfect, forms like אַעֲזִיב are easily recognized. Other Hiphil forms are similar to the Imperfect.

NOTES

1. ר, though not a laryngael, is usually treated as if it were.

2. The Sheva under the laryngael is compounded with the vowel which stands under the preformative letter immediately preceding.

3. When a Sheva stands under the letter immediately following the laryngael, the laryngael itself takes the short vowel of its preformative letter: יַעֲזְבוּ.

VOCABULARY FOR GENESIS 25:27-34

צוּד	to hunt	נָזִיד	meat (for boiling)
צַיִד	hunting, a hunter	עוּף/עָיֵף	to faint
זוּד	to boil	לָעַט	he fed, gave food
אָדֹם/אֲדָמָה	adj. red	בְּכֹרָה	a birthright
מָכַר	he sold	בּוּז/בָּזָה	he despised, spurned
עֲדָשִׁים	lentiles		

vs. 32 הולך למות   "about to die." Note this idiomatic use of the verb הלך to express an idea or an action which is in process or continuation.

vs. 33 השבעה לי   "swear to me." This is a Niphal imperative of שבע. A "paragogic He" has been added for added emphasis.

vs. 34 ויבז   "and [Esau] spurned." You should recognize this form. Here the Vav might well be translated "thus" or "in this manner."

LESSON 31:   THE WEAK PE-ALEPH VERBS

A PE-ALEPH verb may inflect in one of two ways:

1.   It may retain the ALEPH in its Imperfect forms, and function as a PE-Laryngael verb.

2.   The initial ALEPH may quiesce in the forms of the Imperfect. Verbs of this class are called "Weak Pe-Aleph" verbs, and consist mainly in the following words:

אבד   to perish

אכל   to eat

אבה   to be willing

אפה   to bake

אמר   to say

Weak Pe-Aleph verbs are almost regular in the Qal Perfect. The most notable exception is in the plural forms of the second person [אֲכַלְתֶּם/ן] where the laryngael prefers a compound to a simple Shéva. Note also the forms of the Qal Imperative and the Qal Infinitive Construct:

eat!   אֱכֹל, אִכְלִי, אִכְלוּ, אֱכֹלְנָה

[to] eat   [לֶ]אֱכֹל

In the second syllable of the Qal Imperfect, the "o" class vowel never appears, but is replaced by Pataḥ, Ṣere, or Seghol. Quiescent Aleph loses its consonantal force and is silent.

The Qal Participle and Infinitive Absolute inflect in a regular manner. The forms of the Imperfect deserve special attention:

נֹאכַל	אֹכַל
תֹּאכְלוּ	תֹּאכַל
תֹּאכַלְנָה	תֹּאכְלִי
יֹאכְלוּ	יֹאכַל
	תֹּאכַל

אמר

אמר, encountered many times already in the reading exercises, exhibits a special pattern of inflection in the Infinitive Construct, where לֵאמֹר stands instead of לֶאֱמֹר.

לאמר, as you have already seen, often introduces a direct quotation:

דִּבֶּר אַבְרָהָם לֵאמֹר אֲנִי גֵּר בָּאֹהֶל: Abraham spoke, <u>saying</u>, "I live in a tent."

The third person masculine singular form of אמר in the imperfect is יֹאמַר. With the Vav-Consecutive it is sometimes וַיֹּאמֶר and sometimes וַיֹּאמַר. The first form is followed immediately by the words to be spoken, the second is not.

וַיֹּאמַר שְׁמֹר אֶת־הַצֹּאן: And he said, "Watch the sheep!"

וַיֹּאמֶר לוֹ שְׁמֹר אֶת־הַצֹּאן: And he said <u>to him</u>, "Watch the sheep!"

EXERCISE

Below is a list of words which you have already read in Genesis. Be prepared to identify and translate them.

וְאָמְרָה ,וַיֹּאמֶר ,וַתֹּאמֶר ,לֵאמֹר ,לֶאֱכֹל ,לֹא אֹכַל ,וַאֹמַר

לֹא תֹאבֶה ,וְאָמַרְתִּי ,וַיֹּאמְרוּ.

156

מִשְׁמָר an observance, rite   גּוּר to sojourn

עֵקֶב אֲשֶׁר because   רָעָב a famine

רָבָה multiply, be many   לְבַד alone, only

חֹק, חֻקָּה a statute, custom   מִצְוָה a command, precept

שָׁאַל he asked   תּוֹרָה teaching, law

חָרַד he trembled   הָרַג he killed

חָזַק he was strong   עָרַב it was pleasant

גּוֹי a nation   שְׁבֻעָה an oath

NOTE

vs. 3   הָאֵל is written for הָאֵלֶּה.

LESSON 32: THE 'AYIN AND LAMED LARYNGAEL VERBS

'AYIN and LAMED-Laryngael verbs will pose no problem for you if you remember the three general statements made in lesson 30 about the Laryngael letters.

שאל is regular in the Qal Perfect. Note only the third person feminine singular שָׁאֲלָה and the third person plural שָׁאֲלוּ. Remember that the Qal Imperfect will exhibit an "a" thematic vowel (see page 152). The Qal Infinitive Construct and Participles are regular; the Qal Imperative exhibits the "a" thematic vowel apparent also in the forms of the Imperfect:

$$ שָׁאֵל, שַׁאֲלִי, שַׁאֲלוּ, שְׁאַלְנָה $$

שלח, regular in the Qal Perfect, Imperfect, and Imperative, exhibits some important variations in the forms of the infinitives and the participles. This is due to the presence of Pataḥ Furtive (see pages 16 and 17).

Infinitive A: שָׁלוֹחַ   Infinitive C: [לִ]שְׁלוֹחַ

Participle: שֹׁלֵחַ, שֹׁלַחַת, שֹׁלְחִים, שֹׁלְחוֹת

'Ayin and Lamed-Laryngael verbs should be little trouble in the Niphal, Hiphil/Hophal, and Hitpael conjugations if the laryngael rules are remembered (see page 152).

The Piel/Pual stem is affected by the fact that an 'Ayin-Laryngael verb cannot double its middle letter. Note the following characteristic patterns for מִהַר, "he hurried", and מֵאֵן, "he refused".

Perfect:	מִהַרְתִּי	מָאַנְתִּי
	etc.	etc.
Imperfect:	אֲמַהֵר	אֲמָאֵן
	etc.	etc.
Imperative:	מַהֵר	מָאֵן
	מַהֲרִי	מָאֲנִי
	מַהֲרוּ	מָאֲנוּ
	מַהֵרְנָה	מָאֵנָּה
Participle:	מְמַהֵר	מְמָאֵן
	מְמַהֶרֶת	מְמָאֶנֶת
	מְמַהֲרִים	מְמָאֲנִים
	מְמַהֲרוֹת	מְמָאֲנוֹת
Infinitive C:	[לְ]מַהֵר	[לְ]מָאֵן

VOCABULARY FOR GENESIS 26:8-16

בָּקָר	oxen	שַׁעַר	1. a gate
			2. measurement, value
קָנָא	he was jealous	עֲבֻדָּה	[gang of] slaves
חָפַר	he digged	מִקְנֶה	ownership, possession
עָפָר	earth, clay	סתם	Piel: he blocked
שָׁלַח	he sent	עָצַם	he was numerous, strong
שָׁאַל	he asked	אָרַךְ	it was long

159

חַלּוֹן   a window

אַךְ   only, surely

אֵיךְ   how?

צוה   Piel: he commanded

זָרַע   he sowed

כִּמְעַט   easily

שׁקף   he looked [used in Niphal and Hiphil]

צחק   Piel: he joked, made fun/laughter with

אָשָׁם   guilt

נגע   he touched

מָצָא   he found

LESSON 33: THE LAMED-HE AND LAMED-ALEPH VERBS

A large number of Hebrew verbs belong to a class now called "LAMED-HE". That is, they have LAMED as the third root letter. These verbs were originally LAMED-YOD or LA-MED-VAV, but in biblical Hebrew they show HE at the end of a word, standing in place of the original YOD or VAV. The HE indicates the presence of a preceding vowel that is long.

When endings are added to form the Perfect Tense, the original letter often reappears. Note such instances in the paradigms below.

PERFECT

Qal	Niphal	Piel	Hiphil
שָׁתִיתִי	נִשְׁתֵּיתִי	עָשִׂיתִי	הִבְכֵּיתִי
שָׁתִיתָ	נִשְׁתֵּיתָ	עָשִׂיתָ	הִבְכִּיתָ
שָׁתִית	נִשְׁתֵּית	עָשִׂית	הִבְכֵּית
שָׁתָה	נִשְׁתָּה	עָשָׂה	הִבְכָּה
שָׁתְתָה	נִשְׁתְּתָה	עָשְׂתָה	הִבְכְּתָה
שָׁתִינוּ	נִשְׁתֵּינוּ	עָשִׂינוּ	הִבְכִּינוּ
שְׁתִיתֶם	נִשְׁתֵּיתֶם	עֲשִׂיתֶם	הִבְכִּיתֶם
שְׁתִיתֶן	נִשְׁתֵּיתֶן	עֲשִׂיתֶן	הִבְכִּיתֶן
שָׁתוּ	נִשְׁתּוּ	עָשׂוּ	הִבְכּוּ

IMPERFECT

Qal	Niphal	Piel	Hiphil
אֶשְׁתֶּה	אֶשָּׁתֶה	אֲעַשֶּׂה	אַבְכֶּה
תִּשְׁתֶּה	תִּשָּׁתֶה	תְּעַשֶּׂה	תַּבְכֶּה
תִּשְׁתִּי	תִּשָּׁתִי	תְּעַשִּׂי	תַּבְכִּי
יִשְׁתֶּה	יִשָּׁתֶה	יְעַשֶּׂה	יַבְכֶּה
תִּשְׁתֶּה	תִּשָּׁתֶה	תְּעַשֶּׂה	תַּבְכֶּה
נִשְׁתֶּה	נִשָּׁתֶה	נְעַשֶּׂה	נַבְכֶּה
תִּשְׁתּוּ	תִּשָּׁתוּ	תְּעַשּׂוּ	תַּבְכּוּ
תִּשְׁתֶּינָה	תִּשָּׁתֶינָה	תְּעַשֶּׂינָה	תַּבְכֶּינָה
יִשְׁתּוּ	יִשָּׁתוּ	יְעַשּׂוּ	יַבְכּוּ

IMPERATIVE

Qal	Niphal	Piel	Hiphil
שְׁתֵה	הִשָּׁתֵה	עַשֵּׂה	הַבְכֵּה
שְׁתִי	הִשָּׁתִי	עַשִּׂי	הַבְכִּי
שְׁתוּ	הִשָּׁתוּ	עַשּׂוּ	הַבְכּוּ
שְׁתֶינָה	הִשָּׁתֶינָה	עַשֶּׂינָה	הַבְכֶּינָה

PARTICIPLE

Qal	Niphal	Piel	Hiphil
שׁוֹתֶה	נִשְׁתֶּה	מְעַשֶּׂה	מַבְכֶּה
שׁוֹתָה	נִשְׁתֵּית	מְעַשָּׂה	מַבְכָּה
שׁוֹתִים	נִשְׁתִּים	מְעַשִּׂים	מַבְכִּים
שׁוֹתוֹת	נִשְׁתּוֹת	מְעַשּׂוֹת	מַבְכּוֹת

INFINITIVE ABSOLUTE

שָׁתֹה   הִשָּׁתֵֹה   עָשֹׂה   הַבְכֵּה

INFINITIVE CONSTRUCT

[לִ]שְׁתֹות   [לְ]הִשָּׁתֹות   [לַ]עֲשֹׂות   [לְ]הַבְכֹּות

NOTES

1. Most of the Perfect forms can be understood if you remember that the ה of the verb was originally a י.

2. The י, when it precedes afformatives beginning with a consonant, is actually part of a long vowel. The pattern may be either Ḥireq or Ṣere Yod.

3. The third person singular feminine perfect is so written to bring it into apparent conformity with the regular verb.

4. When it precedes afformatives beginning with a vowel, the ה [which was originally a י] is dropped.

5. In the Qal, Lamed-He verbs also exhibit forms of a passive participle:

שָׁתוּי

שְׁתוּיָה

שְׁתוּיִים

שְׁתוּיֹות

LAMED-HE VERBS WITH SPECIAL FORMS

You have already seen the common form וַיְהִי. Many other Lamed-He verbs have special forms in the Imperfect with a Vav-Consecutive or with a Jussive form, both of

which drop the Seghol-He ending. Note carefully the list
of special forms given below. They all occur frequently in
the Hebrew Bible.

Form	Translation	Root
יְהִי	let it [him] be	היה
וַיִּבֶן	and he built	בנה
וַיַּעַל	and he went up	עלה
וַיַּרְא	and he saw	ראה
וַיַּעַשׂ	and he made, did	עשה
וַיַּעַן	and he answered	ענה
וַיֵּבְךְּ	and he wept	בכה
וַיֵּשְׁתְּ	and he drank	שתה
וַתַּהַר	and she conceived	הרה

EXERCISE

Below is a list of words which you have already seen
in a reading passage from Genesis. Be prepared to identify
each form correctly.

וַיְהִי וַיִּרְא יִרְאֶה וַיִּבֶן תַּעַשׂ וַיַּעֲלֵהוּ עֲשִׂיתָ אֲרֻבָּה

תֹּאכְבֶה וַעֲשֵׂה עֲשֵׂה שָׁתָה וְאֶשְׁתֶּה עֲשִׂיתָ לִשְׁתֹּת נָחֲנִי כְּרָאֹת

וְהָיִיתָ וְהָיָה וָאִשֶׁת עֲשִׂים וְאֶפְנֶה וַיַּעַן וַתְּהִי וַיִּשְׁתּוּ

164

LAMED-ALEPH VERBS

Lamed-Aleph verbs are also affected by the quiescence of the Aleph. Whenever, as in the Qal Imperfect of the weak Pe-Alephs, the Aleph loses its force as a consonant, vowel changes occur. Where one would expect יִמְצְא, there is יִמְצָא, the long vowel standing in the open syllable.

The other vocalic changes undergone by Lamed-Aleph verbs should not be too difficult for you to recognize and understand.

SPECIAL NOTES

1. In the derived stems, the thematic vowel may be:

Seghol: תִּמָּצֶאנָה, תְּמַצֶּאנָה, תִּמְצֶאנָה

Ṣere: נִמְצֵאתִי, מִלֵּאתִי, הִמְצֵאתִי

Ḥireq Yod: הִמְצִיא, אַמְצִיא

2. In the Qal Participle, as well as in the Niphal, the Piel, and the Hiphil Participles, the Segholate pattern of the feminine singular undergoes a vowel change.

מְמַלֵּאת מַמְצֵאת נִמְצֵאת מוֹצֵאת

EXERCISE

Below is a list of words which you have already read in Genesis. Be prepared to identify and translate them.

וְאָמְרָה, וַיֹּאמֶר, וַתֹּאמֶר, לֵאמֹר, לֶאֱכֹל, לֹא אָכַל, וָאֹמַר

לֹא תֹאבֶה, וְאָמַרְתִּי, וַיֹּאמְרה.

רֹעֶה	a shepherd		בַּעֲבוּר	.because of, for
פָּרָה	[to] bear fruit		נָטָה	he stretched
חָנָה	he bent, turned, inclined; Hence, he settled down		עָתַק	he moved, was re-moved
נַחַל	a valley, torrent		רָחַב	to be wide, spacious
רִיב	[to] quarrel [with]		פָּרַה	he pierced, digged
אַחֵר	adj. another Fem., אחרת		עָשַׁק	he pressed, grasped; Hence, he oppressed, cheated, defrauded

166

Vocabulary Lessons 30 - 33

צוֹק	חָרֵד	אָפָה
אָשֵׁם	חָזַק	צוּד
נָגַע	גּוֹי	צַיְד
מָצָא	הָרַג	זוּד
רָעֶה	עָרַב	אָדָם אֲדָמָה
פָּרָה	שִׁבְעָה	מָכַר
בַּעֲבוּר	בָּקָר	עֲדָשִׁים
נָטָה	קָנָא	נָזִיד
חָנָה	חָפַר	עִיֵף עָיֵף
נַחַל	עָפָר	לָעַט
רִיב	עֲבֹדָה	בִּכְרָה
אַחֵר	מִקְנֶה	בּוּז בָּזָם
עָתֵק	סָתַם	מִשְׁמָר
רָחָב	עֶצֶם	עָקֵב אֲשֶׁר
פָּרֶה	אָרַך	רָבָה
עָשַׁק	חַלּוֹן	חֹק חֻקָּה
	אַך	שָׁאַל
	אֵיך	גּוּר
	צָוָה	רָעֵב
	זָרַע	לְבַד
	כִּמְעַט	מִצְוָה
	שָׁקַף	תּוֹרָה

167

	PE LARYNGAEL עמד / חזק	'AYIN LARYNG. בחר		LAMED LARYNGAEL שמע / שלח		WEAK PE-ALEPH אמר	LAMED ALEPH מצא	LAMED HE בנה
QAL PERFECT	עָמַד / חָזַק	בָּחַר		שָׁמַע / שָׁלַח		אָמַר	מָצָא	בָּנָה
IMPERF.	יַעֲמֹד / יֶחֱזַק	יִבְחַר		יִשְׁמַע / יִשְׁלַח		יֹאמַר	יִמְצָא	יִבְנֶה
INF. C.	עֲמֹד / חֲזֹק	בְּחֹר		שְׁמֹעַ / שְׁלֹחַ		אֱמֹר	מְצֹא	בְּנוֹת
PART.	עֹמֵד / חָזֵק	בֹּחֵר	פ	שֹׁמֵעַ / שֹׁלֵחַ		אֹמֵר	מֹצֵא	בֹּנֶה
NIPH. PERF.	נֶעֱמַד / נֶחֱזַק	נִבְחַר		נִשְׁמַע / נִשְׁלַח		נֶאֱמַר	נִמְצָא	נִבְנָה
IMPERF.	יֵעָמֵד / יֵחָזֵק	יִבָּחֵר		יִשָּׁמַע / יִשָּׁלַח		יֵאָמֵר	יִמָּצֵא	יִבָּנֶה
INF. C.	הֵעָמֵד / הֵחָזֵק	הִבָּחֵר		הִשָּׁמֵעַ / הִשָּׁלֵחַ		הֵאָמֵר	הִמָּצֵא	הִבָּנוֹת
PART.	נֶעֱמָד / נֶחֱזָק	נִבְחָר		נִשְׁמָע / נִשְׁלָח		נֶאֱמָר	נִמְצָא	נִבְנֶה
PIEL PERFECT				שִׁמַּע / שִׁלַּח	בֵּרַךְ		מִצֵּא	בִּנָּה
IMPERF.				יְשַׁמַּע / יְשַׁלַּח	יְבָרֵךְ		יְמַצֵּא	יְבַנֶּה
INF. C.				שַׁמַּע / שַׁלַּח	בָּרֵךְ		מַצֵּא	בַּנּוֹת
PART.				מְשַׁמֵּעַ / מְשַׁלֵּחַ	מְבָרֵךְ		מְמַצֵּא	מְבַנֶּה
HIPH. PERFECT	הֶעֱמִיד / הֶחֱזִיק	הִבְחִיר		הִשְׁמִיעַ / הִשְׁלִיחַ		הֶאֱמִיר	הִמְצִיא	הִבְנָה
IMPERF.	יַעֲמִיד / יַחֲזִיק	יַבְחִיר		יַשְׁמִיעַ / יַשְׁלִיחַ		יַאֲמִיר	יַמְצִיא	יַבְנֶה
INF. C.	הַעֲמִיד / הַחֲזִיק	הַבְחִיר		הַשְׁמִיעַ / הַשְׁלִיחַ		הַאֲמִיר	הַמְצִיא	הַבְנוֹת
PART.	מַעֲמִיד / מַחֲזִיק	מַבְחִיר		מַשְׁמִיעַ / מַשְׁלִיחַ		מַאֲמִיר	מַמְצִיא	מַבְנֶה

1. LARYNGAELS REJECT DOUBLING, LENGTHEN VOWEL.

2. PREFER A-CLASS VOWELS.

3. COMPOUND INSTEAD OF SIMPLE SHEVA.

4. USE PATAH FURTIVE WITH FINAL ח AND ע (SOMETIMES).

CHARACTERISTICS OF LARYNGAEL VERBS

The three points concerning verbs with Laryngaels (and often Resh) listed on page 152 in effect are the basis for explaining the different vocalizations for these verbs from those of the Strong Verb. The following are observations or comments with these points in mind.

Pe-Laryngael

1. The occurrence of a compound sheva instead of simple sheva is evident in such forms as Qal Perfect 2nd plural (עֲמַדְתֶּם, עֲמַדְתֶּן), Qal Imperfect (יַעֲמֹד, etc; יֶחֱזַק, etc.), Qal Infinitive Construct (עֲמֹד), as well as some forms of the Niphal and Hiphil Stems.

2. The rejected doubling is evident in the Sere as the preformative vowel of the Niphal Imperfect (יֵעָמֵד, etc.), Niphal Imperative (הֵעָמֵד), and Niphal Infinitive Construct (הֵעָמֵד).

3. The preference for a-class vowels is evident in the preformative Pathah as the vowel of יַעֲמֹד; the expected Hireq has become the full vowel of Hateph Pathah due to the influence of the laryngael ʿAyin.

Weak Pe-Aleph

1. Weak Pe-Aleph Verbs are pointed or treated as Pe-Laryngael verbs except in the Qal Imperfect.

2. In the Qal Imperfect, the Aleph quiesces or loses its consonantal force and serves only as the bearer of an o-vowel (יֹאכַל).

ʿAyin Laryngael

The ʿAyin Laryngael verbs show variation from the Strong/Regular verb in the Piel, Pual, and Hitpael stems due to the rejected doubling which lengthens the preformative vowel.

1. Hireq is lengthened to Sere in the Piel Perfect (בֵּרַךְ).

2. Patah is lengthened to Qames in Piel Imperfect (ברך; also Imv. 2ms., בָּרֵךְ), and in the Hitpael (הִתְבָּרֵךְ, etc.)

3. Qibbus is lengthened to Holem in the Pual Perfect (יְבֹרַךְ). and Imperfect (יְבֹרַךְ).

Lamed-Laryngael (ע & ח)

The variation from the Strong or Regular Verb occurs in the vocalization of the ע or ח.

1. The laryngael occurs with a Pathaḥ in the 3m.s. of Qal Imperfect (יִשְׁלַח), of Niphal Imperfect (יִשָּׁלַח), as well as Piel Perfect and Imperfect.

2. A Pathaḥ Furtive occurs with the Qal Act. Participle (שֹׁלֵחַ) as well as with the Hiphil Perfect 3m.s. and Infinitive Construct, and with the Piel, Hiphil, and Hitpael participles.

3. The Pathaḥ occurs instead of Sheva with certain 2nd singular feminine forms (שָׁלַחַתְּ).

Lamed-He

The main characteristics of the Lamed-He Verbs are:

1. The Perfect 3m.s. of all stems have a הָ ending.

2. The Imperfect 3m.s. of all stems have a ה.. ending.

3. The Imperative 2m.s. of all stems have a ה.. ending.

4. The Infinitive Construct of all stems has a וֹת- ending.

5. The Participle (m.s.) of all stems has a ה.. ending.

Lamed-Aleph

The main characteristics of the Lamed-Aleph is that due to the quiescence of the Aleph, there is, in most instances, a lengthening of the accompanying vowel.

LESSON 34: THE NIPHAL OF IRREGULAR VERBS

	Pf.	Impf.	Inf. C.	Ptc.	Imv.
<u>Hollow</u>	נָקוֹם	יִקּוֹם	הִקּוֹם	נָקוֹם	הִקּוֹם
<u>PE-ʾ, PE-ו</u>	נוֹשַׁב	יִוָּשֵׁב	הִוָּשֵׁב	נוֹשָׁב	הִוָּשֵׁב
<u>LAMEDH-HE</u>	נִגְלָה	יִגָּלֶה	הִגָּלוֹת	נִגְלֶה	הִגָּלֵה
<u>PE-NUN</u>	נִגַּשׁ	יִנָּגֵשׁ	הִנָּגֵשׁ	נִגָּשׁ	הִנָּגֵשׁ
<u>PE-ALEPH</u>	נֶאֱכַל	יֵאָכֵל	הֵאָכֵל	נֶאֱכָל	הֵאָכֵל
<u>PE-Laryngael</u>	נֶעֱמַד	יֵעָמֵד	הֵעָמֵד	נֶעֱמָד	הֵעָמֵד
<u>ʿAYIN-Laryn</u>	נִשְׁחַט	יִשָּׁחֵט	הִשָּׁחֵט	נִשְׁחָט	הִשָּׁחֵט
<u>LAMEDH-Laryn</u>	נִשְׁלַח	יִשָּׁלַח	הִשָּׁלַח	נִשְׁלָח	הִשָּׁלַח

LESSON 35: THE HIPHIL OF IRREGULAR VERBS

	Pf.	Impf.	Inf. C.	Ptc.	Imv.
Hollow	הֵקִים	יָקִים	הָקִים	מֵקִים	הָקֵם
PE- י, PE- ו	הוֹשִׁיב	יוֹשִׁיב	הוֹשִׁיב	מוֹשִׁיב	הוֹשֵׁב
LAMEDH-HE	הִגְלָה	יַגְלֶה	הַגְלוֹת	מַגְלֶה	הַגְלֵה
PE-NUN	הִגִּישׁ	יַגִּישׁ	הַגִּישׁ	מַגִּישׁ	הַגֵּשׁ
PE-ALEPH	הֶאֱכִיל	יַאֲכִיל	הַאֲכִיל	מַאֲכִיל	הַאֲכֵל
PE-Laryngael	הֶעֱמִיד	יַעֲמִיד	הַעֲמִיד	מַעֲמִיד	הַעֲמֵד
ʿAYIN-Laryn	הִשְׁאִיל	יַשְׁאִיל	הַשְׁאִיל	מַשְׁאִיל	הַשְׁאֵל
LAMEDH-Laryn	הִשְׁלִיחַ	יַשְׁלִיחַ	הַשְׁלִיחַ	מַשְׁלִיחַ	הַשְׁלַח

VOCABULARY FOR GENESIS 26:26-35

רֵעַ   a friend, companion   שׁכם   Hiph: he rose early

מַדּוּעַ   why?   מִשְׁתֶּה   a banquet

צָבָא	troop, host	שַׂר	master, chief, head
בֵּין־	between	נגד	Hiph: he told
כָּרַת	he cut	מָרָה	bitterness, distress
בְּרִית	a covenant, contract	רוּחַ	spirit, wind, breath
עַל־אֹדוֹת	concerning, about, on account of	נָגַע	he struck, touched

LESSON 36: THE PIEL OF IRREGULAR VERBS

	Pf.	Impf.	Inf. C.	Ptc.	Imv.
Hollow	קוֹמֵם	יְקוֹמֵם	קוֹמֵם	מְקוֹמֵם	קוֹמֵם
PE- , PE-	Regular ....
LAMEDH-HE	גִּלָּה	יְגַלֶּה	גַּלּוֹת	מְגַלֶּה	גַּלֵּה
PE-NUN	Regular ....
PE-ALEPH	Regular ....
PE-Laryngael	Regular ....
⟨AYIN-Laryn	בֵּרַךְ	יְבָרֵךְ	בָּרֵךְ	מְבָרֵךְ	בָּרֵךְ
LAMEDH-Laryn	שִׁלַּח	יְשַׁלַּח	שַׁלַּח	מְשַׁלֵּחַ	שַׁלַּח

NOTE

    The Hollow Verb does not have a Piel form but
rather a "polel." On the analogy of the "Geminate" Verb
(one with the same second and third consonant, e.g., סבב)
the Hollow Verb adds a third consonant when it functions
in the intensive stem.

174

VOCABULARY FOR GENESIS 27:1-12

צֵידָה	venison	קְלָלָה	a curse
תְּלִי	a quiver	גְּדִי	a kid goat
קֶשֶׁת	a bow	עֵז	a she-goat
טַעַם	flavor, taste	חָלָק	smooth
מָשַׁשׁ	he touched, felt	תעע	Pilpel: to sport, jest, mock
כָּהָה	he was weary, feeble, dim of the eyes		

NOTES

vs. 9   אֵהָב is an alternate form of אָהַב.

vs. 11 הֵן is an alternate form of הִנֵּה.

vs. 12 מתעתע is a Pilpel participle of תעע. Geminate verbs
        show Pilpel forms in place of Hitpael ones.

175

LESSON 37: THE HITPAEL OF IRREGULAR VERBS

	Pf.	Impf.	Inf. C.	Ptc.	Imv.
<u>Hollow</u>	הִתְקוֹמֵם	יִתְקוֹמֵם	הִתְקוֹמֵם	מִתְקוֹמֵם	הִתְקוֹמֵם
<u>PE-י, PE-ו</u>	הִתְוַדַּע	יִתְוַדַּע	הִתְוַדַּע	מִתְוַדַּע	הִתְוַדַּע
<u>ʿAYIN Laryn</u>	הִתְבָּרֵךְ	יִתְבָּרֵךְ	הִתְבָּרֵךְ	מִתְבָּרֵךְ	הִתְבָּרֵךְ
<u>LAMEDH-Laryn</u>	הִשְׁתַּלַּח	יִשְׁתַּלַּח	הִשְׁתַּלַּח	מִשְׁתַּלֵּחַ	הִשְׁתַּלַּח

NOTES

The Hitpael Conjugation may be identified easily because of its הִת, יִת, מִת or similar prefix. The only remarkable features appear in the following types of verbs:

1. Hollow verbs, again inflecting on the analogy of the Geminate verbs (see pages 145-146), do not form a "Hitpael," but rather a "Hitpolel."

2. Pe-Yod/Vav verbs re-introduce the initial Vav following the preformative letters.

3. ברך reveals the lengthened vowel necessary when the double letter of a verb refuses doubling.

4. שׁלח, a Lamed-Laryngael verb, also shows the effects of metathesis (see page 123).

VOCABULARY FOR GENESIS 27:13-24

חֲמֻדֹת   pleasant things

עוֹר   skin [animal or human]

קרה   Qal: he met; Hiph: he caused to meet

לָבַשׁ   he put on [clothes]

צַוָּאר   the neck

נכר   Qal: he knew;
הִכִּיר   Hiph: he recognized

NOTES

vs. 19   שְׁבָה is a Qal imperative form of ישׁב with paragogic ה added for emphasis.

vs. 21   גְּשָׁה is a Qal imperative form of נגשׁ with paragogic ה once again added for emphasis. This is a common occurrence.

LESSON 38: ADDITIONAL INFORMATION ON THE HEBREW NOUN

NOUNS WITH PREFORMATIVE LETTERS

Many nouns in Hebrew are formed from the root con-
sonants of a verb by the addition of a preformative letter.
The letters which are most often used in this manner are
Aleph, Mem, and Tav. In all the charts below, the forms
of each word are given in the following order: Absolute
Singular, Construct Singular, Absolute Plural, Construct
Plural.

א

cluster (m)	אֶשְׁכּוֹל	־אֶשְׁכּוֹל	אֶשְׁכֹּלוֹת	־אֶשְׁכְּלוֹת
native (m)	אֶזְרָח	־אֶזְרַח		
finger (f)	אֶצְבַּע	־אֶצְבַּע	אֶצְבָּעוֹת	־אֶצְבְּעוֹת

מ

wilderness (m)	מִדְבָּר	־מִדְבַּר
key (m)	מַפְתֵּחַ	־מַפְתֵּחַ

judgment (m)	מִשְׁפָּט	מִשְׁפַּט־	מִשְׁפָּטִים	מִשְׁפָּטֵי־
family (f)	מִשְׁפָּחָה	מִשְׁפַּחַת־	מִשְׁפָּחוֹת	מִשְׁפְּחוֹת־
tabernacle (m)	מִשְׁכָּן	מִשְׁכַּן־	מִשְׁכָּנוֹת	מִשְׁכְּנֵי־/וֹת־
altar (m)	מִזְבֵּחַ	מִזְבַּח־	מִזְבְּחוֹת	

ת

desire, wish (f)	תַּאֲוָה	תַּאֲוַת־		
thanksgiving (f)	תּוֹדָה	תּוֹדַת־	תּוֹדוֹת	תּוֹדֹת־
instruction (f)	תּוֹרָה	תּוֹרַת־	תּוֹרוֹת	תּוֹרֹת־
hope (f)	תִּקְוָה	תִּקְוַת־		
generations (f)			תּוֹלְדוֹת	תּוֹלְדֹת־

NOUNS WITH SUFFORMATIVE LETTERS

Certain Hebrew nouns are formed by the addition of Lamed, Mem, or Nun as afformatives. Abstract endings like ִית, וֹת, and וּת may also be considered in this class.

garden (m)	כַּרְמֶל		
majesty (m)	גָּאוֹן	גְּאוֹן־	
offering (m)	קָרְבָּן	קָרְבַּן־	
table (m)	שֻׁלְחָן	שֻׁלְחַן־	שֻׁלְחָנוֹת
kingdom (f)	מַלְכוּת	מַלְכוּת־	מַלְכֻיּוֹת
remnant (f)	שְׁאֵרִית	שְׁאֵרִית־	
instant, suddenness (m)	פִּתְאוֹם		

NOUNS WITH MORE THAN THREE-LETTERED ROOTS

אַרְגָּמָן	purple, red-purple;	Root:	רגמן
כַּרְכֹּב	border, rim [of altar];	Root:	כרכב
כַּפְתּוֹר	capital, knob;	Root:	כפתר
צְפַרְדֵּעַ	frog;	Root:	צפרדע

NOUNS OF REDUPLICATION

עַפְעַפַּיִם	eyelash;	Root:	עוף
צֶאֱצָאִים	offspring, produce;	Root:	יצא
קָדְקֹד	head, crown of head;	Root:	קדד

COLLECTIVE NOUNS

בְּהֵמָה	cattle
בָּקָר	oxen, herd
עוֹף	birds, a bird
עֵץ	trees, woods, a tree
דָּגָן	grain

VOCABULARY FOR GENESIS 27:25-46

אֵבֶל	mourning	אֲחָדִים	a few

אֶחָד	one; Fem: אַחַת	אַף	nose, anger
אֵפוֹא	consequently, now	נָשַׁק	he kissed
אָצַל	he reserved, put aside	סָמַךְ	he leaned [upon]
אָרַר	he cursed	עוֹל	a yoke
בָּרַח	he fled	עָקַב	he deceived
בְּרָכָה	a benediction, blessing	פָּרַק	he broke off, tore to pieces
דָּגָן	grain	צָעַק	he cried, shrieked
חֵמָה	anger, burning	צְעָקָה	a cry [of anguish]
חֶרֶב	a sword	קוּץ	to loathe
חָרַד	he trembled	רוּד	Qal & Hiph: to rove, be restless
חֲרָדָה	terror, trembling	רוּחַ	to smell
טַל	dew	רֵיחַ	scent, fragrance, smell
יַיִן	wine	שׁוּב	to turn, return
לְמַעַן	in order [that]	שָׁכַח	he forgot
מַטְעָם	tasty food	שָׁכֹל	he was bereaved
מַר, מָרָה	bitter, strong	שֶׁמֶן	oil, fatness, land-fertility
מִרְמָה	deceit	תִּירוֹשׁ	new, unfermented wine
נחם	Niph: to pity, have compassion; Piel: to console, comfort; Hit: to feel compassion, comfort oneself		

LESSON 39: HEBREW NUMBERS

1 - 10

The Hebrew numbers from one through ten exhibit the following forms:

MASCULINE			FEMININE		
Abs.		Con.	Abs.		Con.
אֶחָד [or חַד]		אַחַד	אַחַת [or אֶחָת]		אַחַת
שְׁנַיִם		שְׁנֵי	שְׁתַּיִם		שְׁתֵּי
שְׁלֹשָׁה		שְׁלֹשֶׁת	שָׁלֹשׁ		שְׁלֹשׁ
אַרְבָּעָה		אַרְבַּעַת	אַרְבַּע		אַרְבַּע
חֲמִשָּׁה		חֲמֵשֶׁת	חָמֵשׁ		חֲמֵשׁ
שִׁשָּׁה		שֵׁשֶׁת	שֵׁשׁ		שֵׁשׁ
שִׁבְעָה		שִׁבְעַת	שֶׁבַע		שְׁבַע
שְׁמֹנָה		שְׁמֹנַת	שְׁמֹנֶה		שְׁמֹנֶה
תִּשְׁעָה		תִּשְׁעַת	תֵּשַׁע		תְּשַׁע
עֲשָׂרָה		עֲשֶׂרֶת	עֶשֶׂר		עֶשֶׂר

182

1. Construct forms always precede the noun with which they are used.

אַחַד הֶהָרִים   one of the mountains

שְׁתֵּי נָשִׁים   two women

2. The absolute forms normally precede the noun also.

שְׁלֹשָׁה בָתִּים   three houses

שֶׁבַע שָׁנִים   seven years

3. The number one in the absolute state always <u>follows</u> its noun.

אִישׁ אֶחָד   one man

אִשָּׁה אַחַת   one woman

4. The plural form of אֶחָד is אֲחָדִים, which means "a few" or "several."

5. The number two is used in the absolute state only without a noun. Cf. Amos 3:3:

הֲיֵלְכוּ שְׁנַיִם יַחְדָּו   "Do two [men] walk together?"

11 - 19

The numbers eleven through nineteen exhibit the forms listed below, all of which precede the noun. The noun used with these numbers is usually plural but may be singular if it is an oft-used word.

MASCULINE	FEMININE
אַחַד עָשָׂר	אַחַת עֶשְׂרֵה
שְׁנַיִם עָשָׂר	שְׁתֵּים עֶשְׂרֵה
שְׁלֹשָׁה עָשָׂר	שְׁלֹשׁ עֶשְׂרֵה

אַרְבַּע עֶשְׂרֵה	אַרְבָּעָה עָשָׂר
חֲמֵשׁ עֶשְׂרֵה	חֲמִשָּׁה עָשָׂר
שֵׁשׁ עֶשְׂרֵה	שִׁשָּׁה עָשָׂר
שְׁבַע עֶשְׂרֵה	שִׁבְעָה עָשָׂר
שְׁמוֹנֶה עֶשְׂרֵה	שְׁמוֹנָה עָשָׂר
תְּשַׁע עֶשְׂרֵה	תִּשְׁעָה עָשָׂר

The number eleven has the alternate forms עַשְׁתֵּי עָשָׂר (m)
and עַשְׁתֵּי עֶשְׂרֵה (f). Twelve has the alternate forms שְׁנֵי עָשָׂר (m)
and שְׁתֵּי עֶשְׂרֵה (f).

20 - 99

Before reading the chart of these numbers below, note
the following important facts: First, the numbers twenty,
thirty, etc., exhibit only one form for both masculine and
feminine nouns. Second, the numbers one through nine, when
used with an even multiple of ten to form a compound number,
are inflected to agree with the noun modified. Third, the
noun modified may be either singular or plural, but is more
often singular for these numbers. Example: עֶשְׂרִים וּשְׁנַיִם אִישׁ
twenty-two men.

עֶשְׂרִים	twenty
שְׁלֹשִׁים	thirty
אַרְבָּעִים	forty
חֲמִשִּׁים	fifty
שִׁשִּׁים	sixty
שִׁבְעִים	seventy
שְׁמוֹנִים	eighty
תִּשְׁעִים	ninety

The following list shows the way in which larger numbers
are expressed in Biblical Hebrew. Note that for compounds the
order of listing is from large to small. Thus 9,999 is written
תִּשְׁעַת אֲלָפִים תְּשַׁע מֵאוֹת תִּשְׁעִים וָתֵּשַׁע.

100	מֵאָה
200	מָאתַיִם
300	שְׁלֹשׁ מֵאוֹת
400	אַרְבַּע מֵאוֹת
500	חֲמֵשׁ מֵאוֹת
600	שֵׁשׁ מֵאוֹת
700	שְׁבַע מֵאוֹת
800	שְׁמוֹנֶה מֵאוֹת
900	תְּשַׁע מֵאוֹת
1000	אֶלֶף
2000	אַלְפַּיִם
3000	שְׁלֹשֶׁת אֲלָפִים
4000	אַרְבַּעַת אֲלָפִים
5000	חֲמֵשֶׁת אֲלָפִים
6000	שֵׁשֶׁת אֲלָפִים
7000	שִׁבְעַת אֲלָפִים
8000	שְׁמוֹנַת אֲלָפִים
9000	תִּשְׁעַת אֲלָפִים
10000	עֲשֶׂרֶת אֲלָפִים

Note that the number ten-thousand may also be expressed
by the words רְבָבָה and רִבּוֹא.

ORDINAL NUMBERS

The following chart lists the masculine and feminine
forms of the ordinal numbers.

M	F	
רִאשׁוֹן	רִאשׁוֹנָה	first
שֵׁנִי	שֵׁנִית, שְׁנִיָּה	second
שְׁלִישִׁי	שְׁלִישִׁית	third
רְבִיעִי	רְבִיעִית	fourth
חֲמִישִׁי	חֲמִישִׁית	fifth
שִׁשִּׁי	שִׁשִּׁית	sixth
שְׁבִיעִי	שְׁבִיעִית	seventh
שְׁמִינִי	שְׁמִינִית	eighth
תְּשִׁיעִי	תְּשִׁיעִית	ninth
עֲשִׂירִי	עֲשִׂירִית	tenth
הָאַחַד עָשָׂר	הָאַחַת עֶשְׂרֵה	eleventh
הַשְּׁנֵים עָשָׂר	הַשְּׁתֵּים עֶשְׂרֵה	twelvth

etc.....................

Note that above ten, the cardinal numbers become
ordinal by prefixing the article.

FRACTIONS

Biblical Hebrew uses the following fractions:

חֲצִי, חֵצִי, מֶחֱצָה, מַחֲצִית	one-half
רֹבַע, רֶבַע	one-fourth
חֹמֶשׁ	one-fifth

LESSON 40: THE HEBREW BIBLE

The Hebrew Bible consists of three major divisions, called in Hebrew תורה, נביאים, and כתובים. From the first letter of each of these divisions comes the abbreviation תנ"ך, the common Hebrew word for "Bible."

Counting only one book for Samuel, Kings, Chronicles, The Twelve Minor Prophets, and Ezra-Nehemiah, the Hebrew Bible totals twenty-four books instead of the English thirty-nine. Further, the order of the books in each section of the Hebrew text varies from the well-known sequence adopted for English versions of the Bible. In addition, the Hebrew names of each book are often quite different from the ones known in English. This is so because the Hebrew and English names stem from different sources. Hebrew relies either on the first (important) word or phrase in a book or upon the name of a major character therein for its title. English, depending upon either Greek or Latin titles, uses names that try to describe the contents of a book or to name a major character therein.

Below is a list of the twenty-four books of the Hebrew Bible, given in their Hebrew order. Accompanying each is a translation of the Hebrew title and the English equivalent title taken from Greek or Latin.

תורה

בראשית	"In [the] beginning ..."	GENESIS
שמות	"[These are] the names ..."	EXODUS
ויקרא	"Then [God] called ..."	LEVITICUS

במדבר	"In the [Sinai] desert ..."	NUMBERS
דברים	"[These are] the things ..."	DEUTERONOMY

נביאים

The "prophetic" section of the Hebrew Bible divides into two parts, נביאים האחרונים and נביאים הראשונים, or "Former Prophets" and "Latter Prophets." In the list below the first four books are "former" and the remaining four are "latter." The Hebrew names of the twelve "Minor Prophets" are: הושע, יואל, עמוס, עובדיה, יונה, מיכה, נחום, חבקוק, צפניה, חגי, זכריה, מלאכי. Remember that they form only one book in the Hebrew Bible, called "The Twelve" (שנים עשר).

יהושע	JOSHUA
שופטים	JUDGES
שמואל	SAMUEL
מלכים	KINGS
ישעיה	ISAIAH
ירמיה	JEREMIAH
יחזקאל	EZEKIEL
שנים עשר	THE TWELVE

כתובים

תהלים	"Praises"	PSALMS
משלי		PROVERBS
איוב		JOB
שיר השירים		SONG OF SONGS

189

רות		RUTH
איכה	How!	LAMENTATIONS
קהלת	Collector (of sentences)	ECCLESIASTES
אסתר		ESTHER
דניאל		DANIEL
עזרא נחמיה		EZRA-NEHEMIAH
דברי הימים	"The words of the days"	CHRONICLES

רַע	חֲמֻדוֹת	מִרְמָה
מַדּוּעַ	עוֹר	נחם
שְׁכֶם	קָרָה	אַף
מִשְׁתֶּה	לָבַשׁ	נֶשֶׁק
צָבָא	צַוָּאר	סָמַךְ
בִּין	נכר	עוֹל
כָּרַת	הִפִּיר	עָקֵב
בְּרִית	אֵבֶל	פָּרַק
עַל־אֹדוֹת	אֲחֻדָיהָ	צָעַק
שַׂר	אֶחָד	צְעָקָה
נגד	אֵפוֹא	קוּץ
מָרָה	אֵצֶל	רוּד
רוּחַ	אָרַר	רוּחַ
נָגַע	פרח	רֵיחַ
צֵידָה	בְּרָכָה	שׁוּב
תְּלִי	דָּגָן	שָׁכַח
קֶשֶׁת	חֵמָה	שָׂכַל
טַעַם	חֶרֶב	שֶׁמֶן
מָשָׁשׁ	חָרַד	תִּירוֹשׁ
כָּהָה	חֲרָדָה	
קְלָלָה	טַל	
גְּדִי	יַיִן	
עֵז	לְמַעַן	
חָלָק	מַטְעַם	
תעע	מָר, מָרָה	

191

GLOSSARY

For verbs, the second form listed is the Imperfect.
For nouns and adjectives, alternate, feminine, or plural
forms are sometimes listed.

א

אָב   אָבוֹת   father, ancestor, m.

אבד   יֹאבַד   perish

אבה   יֹאבֶה   be willing

אֵבֶל   mourning, m.

אברהם   Abraham

אָדוֹן   lord, master, m.

אֱדֹם   Edom.

אָדֹם   אֲדָמָה   adj. red

אַדְמוֹנִי   adj. red-haired, ruddy

אֶדֶר   splendor, a cloak (?), m.

אהב   יאהב   love

אֹהֶל   tent, m.

אוֹ   or

אוה   desire, long for

אָז   adv. then

אֶזְרָח   native, m.

אֹזֶן   ear, f

אָח   brother, m.

אֶחָד   one, m.

אֲחָדִים   a few

אָחוֹת   sister, f.

אחז   יֹאחֵז   seize

אַחַר   after

אַחֵר   אֲחֵרוֹת, אֲחֵרִים, אַחֶרֶת   adj. other

אַחֲרֵי   after;   אַחֲרֵי כֵן   afterwards, after this.

אַחַת   one, f.

אֹיֵב   enemy, m.

אַיֵּה   where (is)?

אֵיךְ   how?

אַיִל   ram, hart, m.

אִישׁ   אֲנָשִׁים   man.

אַךְ   adv. only, surely, doubtlessly

אכל   יֹאכַל   eat

אֹכֶל   food, m;   אָכְלָה   food, f.

אַל   no, not.

אֶל   to(ward),   passim.

אָלָה   oath, curse, f.

אֵלֶּה   these, m or f.

194

אֱלֹהִים		God
אֻלַי		perhaps
אֶלֶף		one-thousand
אִם		if
אֵם	אִמּוֹת	mother, f.
אֻמָּה		a family, tribe, f.
אמץ	יֶאֱמַץ	be powerful, courageous
אמר	יֹאמַר	say
אֱמֶת		truth, f.
אֲנַחְנוּ		we
אֱנוֹשׁ		man, mankind
אֲנִי	אָנֹכִי	I
אֳנִיָּה		a ship, vessel, f.
אסף	יֶאֱסֹף	gather
אַף	אַפַּיִם	nose, face, anger, m.
אפה	יֹאפֶה	bake
אֵפוֹא		consequently, now
אֶצְבַּע		finger, f.
אצל		he reserved, put aside
אפק	יִתְאַפַּק	restrain oneself
אַרְבַּע	four; אַרְבָּעִים	forty
אַרְגָּמָן		purple, red-purple, m.
אַרְיֵה		lion, m.
ארך		be long
אֶרֶץ	אֲרָצוֹת	a land, country, f.
ארר		curse

אֵשׁ   fire, f.

אִשָּׁה   נָשִׁים   woman, f.

אֲשֶׁר   relative pronoun: who, which, that

אַתְּ   you, sg., f.

אֵת   אֶת an untranslatable particle used to indicate a definite direct object

אַתָּה   you, sg., m.

אַתֶּם   you, pl., m.

אֶתְמוֹל   yesterday

אַתֵּן   אַתֵּנָה you, pl., f.

ב

בְּ   in, with, by,   בַּ/בָּ in the.

בְּאֵר   a well, f.

בֶּגֶד   a garment, m.

בְּהֵמָה   cattle

בּוֹא   to come

בזה   בוז to despise, spurn

בֶּטֶן   belly, womb, f.

בֵּין   between

בַּיִת   בָּתִּים house, m.

בכה   יִבְכֶּה weep   Hiph: be sad.

בְּכֹר   first-born, m.

בְּכֹרָה   birthright, f.

בֵּן   בָּנִים   a son

בֶּן־יַעֲקֹב   Jacob's son

בנה   יִבְנֶה   build

בַּעֲבוּר   for, because of

בַּעַל   lord, owner, Baal

בקע   cut, split, divide

בֶּקַע   half, m.

בָּקָר   herd, oxen, cattle

בֹּקֶר   morning, m.

ברא   יִבְרָא   create

ברח   יִבְרַח   flee

בְּרִית   a covenant, contract, f.

ברך   Qal: to kneel, bend the knee   Piel:
to bless

בְּרָכָה   a blessing, benediction, f.

בַּת   בָּנוֹת   a daughter, f.

ג

גָּאוֹן   majesty, pride, m.

גִּבּוֹר   warrior, m.

גְּבֻל   border, boundary, m.

גָּג   roof, m.   Plural: גַּגּוֹת

גָּד   Gad

גָּדוֹל   adj. large, big, old, great

גְּדִי   a goat, kid, m.

גדל   יִגְדַּל   be great, grow up

גּוֹי   a people, nation, m.

גוע   יִגְוַע   expire, die

גוּר   to sojourn, dwell

גַּם   also

גמא   Hiph: give (someone) a drink

גָּמָל   a camel, m.

ד

דבר   יְדַבֵּר   Piel: speak

דָּבָר   דְּבָרִים   a word, thing, matter, m.

דָּג   a fish, m.

דָּגָן   grain, m.

דָּן   Dan

דֶּלֶת   a door, f.

דֶּרֶךְ   a road, way, path, m. or f.

דרש   יִדְרֹשׁ   ask, inquire

ה

הַ   question marker

198

הַ, הָ, הֶ   "the" (definite article)

הגה   יֶהְגֶּה   meditate

הוּא   he, it (personal pronoun); that (demonstrative)

הִיא   she, it (personal pronoun); that (demonstrative)

היה   יִהְיֶה   to be

הֵיכָל   temple, m.

הלך   יֵלֵךְ   go, walk

הֵם   הֵמָּה   they, m; those

הֵן   הֵנָּה   they, f; those

הִנֵּה   here is, behold

הָר   הָרִים   a mountain

הרג   יַהֲרֹג   kill

הרה   יֶהֱרֶה   conceive, become pregnant   Cf.
        וַתַּהַר: "Then she conceived ..."

ו

וְ, וַ, וָ, וּ   and

וַשְׁתִּי   Vashti, wife of King Ahasuerus

ז

זֹאת   this, f.

זֶה   this, m.

199

זָהָב   gold, m.

זוּד   to boil

זָקֵן   יִזְקַן   be old

זָקֵן   זְקֵנָה   adj. old

זִקְנָה   oldness, f.

זרע   יִזְרַע   sow

ח

חֶבְרוֹן   Hebron

חבש   יַחֲבֹשׁ   saddle, bind around

חַג   חַגִּים   a festival, feast, m.

חוֹל   חוֹלוֹת   sand, mud, m.

חוּץ   מִחוּץ   outside

חָזָק   adj. strong

חַיִּים   life, lifetime, m. pl.

חָכָם   wise, wise person

חֲלוֹם   חֲלוֹמוֹת   a dream, m.

חַלּוֹן   חַלּוֹנוֹת   a window, m.

חלם   יַחֲלֹם   dream

חָלָק   adj. smooth

חֲמָדוֹת   pleasant things

חֲמוֹר   חֲמוֹרִים   donkey, m.

חָמֵשׁ   five, f.

חנה   bend, turn, incline; hence, settle down

חֶ֫סֶד   covenant faithfulness

חפר   וַיַּחְפֹּר   dig

חָצֵר   a village, m.

חֹק   חֻקָּה   a statute, custom, law, m.

חֶ֫רֶב   a sword, f.

חרד   tremble

חֲרָדָה   terror, trembling,

חרה   יֶחֱרֶה   be, become enraged

ט

טבח   יִטְבַּח   slaughter, slay (sacrificial animal)

טוב   טֹבוֹת, טוֹבִים, טוֹבָה   adj. good

טִירָה   טִירוֹת   an encampment, f.

טַל   dew, m.

טַ֫עַם   flavor, taste, m.

טֶ֫רֶם   adv. before

י

יָד   יַדַיִם, יָדוֹת   a hand, f.

ידע   יָדַע   know

יְהוּדָה   Judah

יוֹם	יָמִים	day, m.
יוֹסֵף		Joseph
יַחַד		together
יַחְדָּו		together
יטב	יִיטַב	be good · Not used in the Perfect
יַיִן		wine, m.
יכח		Hiph: decide
יכל	יוּכַל	be able
ילד	יָלַד	Qal: bear (a child), beget; Hiph: הוֹלִיד, יוֹלִיד father (a child); Niph: נוֹלַד, הִוָּלֵד[לְ] be born
יֶלֶד	יְלָדִים	boy, m.
יַלְדָּה	ילדות	girl, f.
יָם		sea, West, m.
יָמִין		right (hand)
יסף	וַיֹּסֶף	add, increase
יִצְחָק		Isaac
ירא	יִירָא	be afraid
ירד	יֵרֵד	descend, go down
יְרוּשָׁלַיִם		Jerusalem
יָרֵךְ		thigh, m.
ירש	יִירַשׁ	inherit, possess
יֵשׁ		there is, there are
ישב	יֵשֵׁב	dwell, sit
ישר	יִישַׁר	be upright, righteous

כְּ   as, like

כבד   יִכְבַּד   be heavy, rich, respected

כַּד   jar (for water), f.

כֹּה   thus

כהה   be weary, feeble, faint, dim of eye

כּוֹכָב   star, m.

כִּי   for, because

כֹּל   all, each, every

כלה   יִכְלֶה   finish, cease, end

כְּלִי   כֵּלִים   vessel, utensil, tool, m.

כִּמְעַט   easily

כְּנַעַן   Canaan

כָּנָף   wing, f.

כסה   cover

כֶּסֶף   silver, money, m.

כַּפְתּוֹר   capital, knob, m.

כרה   יִכְרֶה   pierce, dig

כַּרְכֹּב   border, rim (of altar), m.

כַּרְמֶל   garden, m.

כרת   יִכְרֹת   cut

כתב   יִכְתֹּב   write

לְ	to, for; לְ also indicates possession, and serves as a sign of the infinitive construct, 1, 8, passim
לֹא	no, not
לְאֹם	a people, nation
לֵאמֹר	"saying;" used to introduce a direct quotation
לֵב	לֵבָב heart, m.
לְבַד	alone, only
לבש	put on (clothes)
לֶחֶם	bread, food
לַיְלָה	לֵילוֹת night, m.
לִין	לוּן to spend the night
לְמַעַן	in order (that)
לְנֹכַח	in behalf of
לִפְנֵי	before, in the presence of, facing
לקח	יִקַּח take
לקט	יִלְקֹט gather, pick up

מ

מֵאָה	one-hundred
מַאֲכֶלֶת	a knife, f.
מֵאֵת	prep. from
מִגְדָּנָה	precious thing, f.

מִדְבָּר   wilderness, desert, m.

מַדּוּעַ   why?

מהר   Piel: hurry

מוֹלֶדֶת   kinfolk, relatives, f.

מוֹרֶה   מוֹרֶה a teacher, instructor

מוּת   to die

מָוֶת   death,   Construct: מוֹת.

מִזְבֵּחַ   מִזְבְּחוֹת an altar, place of sacrifice, m.

מָחָר   adv. tomorrow

מַחֲרִישׁ   adv. silently

מַטְעַם   tasty food

מִי   who?

מַיִם   water, m, pl.

מֵינֶקֶת   a nurse, f.

מלא   יִמְלָא be full,   Piel: fill (something).

מַלְאָךְ   messenger, angel, m.

מֶלֶךְ   king, m.

מַלְכוּת   kingdom, f.

מִן   from

מִסְפּוֹא   fodder

מֵעָה   intestines, belly, f.

מְעַט   a little

מְעָרָה   a cave, bare place, f.

מצא   יִמְצָא find

מִצְוָה   a command, precept, f.

מִצְרַיִם   Egypt

מָקוֹם   מְקוֹמוֹת   a place, m.

מִקְנֶה   ownership, possession, m.

מַפְתֵּחַ   a key, m.

מַר   מָרָה   adj. bitter, strong

מֹרָה   bitterness, distress

מִרְמָה   deceit, f.

מִשְׁכָּן   a tabernacle, m.

משל   rule (over), be in charge

מִשְׁמָר   an observance, rite, m.

מִשְׁפָּחָה   a family, f.

מִשְׁפָּט   מִשְׁפָּטִים   justice, judgment, m.

מִשְׁקָל   a weight, m.

משש   touch, feel

מִשְׁתֶּה   a banquet, m.

מֵת   מֵתָה   adj. dead

מַתָּנָה   a gift, f.

נ

נָבִיא   נְבִיאִים   a prophet, m.

נֶגֶב   the Negev, South

נגד   Hiph: הִגִּיד, יַגִּיד   tell, make known

נגש   יִגַּשׁ   come near, approach

נגע   יִגַּע   touch

נָזִיד	a boiled dish, m.
נחה	guide, lead
נֶזֶם	a nose ring, m.
נַחַל	a torrent, a valley, m.
נחם	Piel: to pity, have compassion; Hiph: to console, comfort; Hit: to feel compassion, (seek to) comfort oneself.
נטה	יִטֶּה, וַיֵּט extend, stretch out
נכר	Qal: know; Hiph: הִכִּיר recognize, acknowledge
נָכְרִי	נָכְרִיָּה adj. foreign, strange
נסה	Piel: to test
נַעַר	a young man, נַעֲרָה a young woman
נפל	יִפֹּל fall
נצב	Niph: be stationed, standing
נקה	be innocent, clean, free
נָקִי	נְקִיָּה adj. free, not obligated
נשא	יִשָּׂא raise, lift up
נָשִׁים	women. See אִשָּׁה.
נשק	יִשַּׁק kiss

ס

סבב	יָסֹב to turn, go around
סָבִיב	around, surrounding,
סֹבֶךְ	a thicket, m.
סוס	סוּסוֹת, סוּסִים, סוּסָה a horse, mare

207

סֹחֵר סֹחֲרִים a merchant, m.

ספר Qal: to count; Piel: tell, recount

סֵפֶר a book

סמך lean (upon)

סתם Piel: to block, stop up

ע

עבד יַעֲבֹד work, serve

עֶבֶד עֲבָדִים servant, slave

עֲבֻדָּה (gang of) slaves

עֲבוֹדָה work, f.

עַד unto,   עַד־אִם until

עֲדָשִׁים lentiles

עוֹד yet, still, another

עוֹל a yoke, m.

עוֹף a bird, fowl, birds, m

עוֹר skin (animal or human)

עַז עַזָּה adj. strong

עֵז עִזִּים a she-goat, f.

עזב יַעֲזֹב forsake, leave

עַיִן an eye, a fountain; עֲיָנוֹת fountains; עֵינַיִם
eyes (plural and dual), f.

עָיֵף עֲיֵפָה adj. faint, exhausted

עִיר עָרִים a city, f.

208

עַל   on, upon, near   עַל אֹדוֹת   concerning, about, on account of

עלה   יַעֲלֶה   go up, ascend

עַלְמָה   עֲלָמוֹת   a young lady, f.

עַם   עַמִּים   people

עִם   with,

עמד   יַעֲמֹד   stand

ענה   יַעֲנֶה   answer

עַפְעַפַּיִם   eyelash

עָפָר   earth, clay, m.

עֵץ   עֵצִים   tree(s), wood, m.

עצם   be mighty, vast, numerous

עקב   deceive

עָקֵב   a heel, m.

עֵקֶב   עֵקֶב אֲשֶׁר   because

עקד   bind

עָקָר   עֲקָרָה   adj. sterile, barren

ערב   be pleasant

עֶרֶב   evening, m.

ערה   empty

ערך   יַעֲרֹךְ   put in rows, arrange

עשה   יַעֲשֶׂה   do, make

עׁשׁק   Hit: oppress, cheat, defraud

עֲשָׂרָה   ten, m.

עָשִׁיר   adj. rich

עֵת   time, f.

עַתָּה   adv. now

עתק   יֵעָתֵק   move, remove

עתר   יֵעָתֵר   entreat

פ

פֶּה   פֵּיוֹת   mouth, m.

פֹּה   here

פִּילֶגֶשׁ   a concubine, f.

פֶּן   lest

פָּנִים   a face, countenance, front, m and f.   See לִפְנֵי

פעל   יִפְעַל   to work

פַּעַם   a time, once; פַּעֲמַיִם twice; Pl: פְּעָמִים, f.

פרד   be separated

פרה   יִפְרֶה   bear fruit, be fruitful

פרץ   break off, through

פִּתְאֹם   suddenness, instant.   Used as an adverbial accusative to mean "suddenly."

פתח   Qal: to open; Piel: to unload (an animal)

צ

צֹאן   small cattle, sheep, flock, f/coll.

צֶאֱצָאִים   offspring, produce

צָבָא   צְבָאוֹת   a troop, host, army, m.

צַוָּאר   the neck, m.

צוד   יָצוּד   to hunt

צוה   וַיְצַו   Piel: to command, order

צחק   Piel: to joke, make fun, laugh with

צַיִד   hunting, a hunter, m.

צֵידָה   venison

צלח   Hiph: to prosper, succeed

צמא   be thirsty

צָמִיד   a bracelet, m.

צָעִיף   a veil, m.

צעק   cry, shriek

צְעָקָה   a cry (of anguish), f.

צָעִיר   adj. small, young

צָפוֹן   North

צִפּוֹר   a bird, m·

צְפַרְדֵּעַ   a frog, m.

ק

קבר   יִקְבֹּר   to bury

קֶבֶר   a grave, m.

קדד   יִקֹּד   bow the head

קָדוֹשׁ   adj. holy

211

קֶדֶם   East

קָדְקוֹד   head, crown (of head), m.

קוֹל   קוֹלוֹת   sound, voice, m

קוּם   יָקוּם   to arise, get up,   Cf. ויקם.

קוּץ   יָקוּץ   to loathe, hate greatly

קָטֹן   יִקְטַן   be small, young, unimportant

קָטָן   קְטַנָּה, קָטֹן   adj. small, young, unimportant

קנא   be jealous

קְלָלָה   a curse, f.

קנה   יִקְנֶה   buy, acquire

קרא   יִקְרָא   call, read,   happen, occur

קָרְבָּן   an offering, m.

קרה   meet, encounter; Hiph: cause to meet, cause to happen. See קרא.

קָרוֹב   adj. near, close

קֶרֶן   a horn, f.

קָשֶׁה   קָשָׁה, קָשִׁים, קָשׁוֹת   adj. hard, difficult

קֶשֶׁת   קְשָׁתוֹת   a bow, rainbow, f.

ר

ראה   יראה   to see

רֹאשׁ   רָאשִׁים   head, top, summit

רִאשׁוֹן   רִאשׁוֹנָה   adj. first, former

212

רַב   רַבָּה   adj. much, many, numerous

רְבָבָה   myriad, ten-thousand, f.

רבה   יִרְבֶּה   multiply, become great, numerous

רֶגֶל   a foot, f.

רדף   יִרְדֹּף   pursue, chase

רוד   יָרוּד   Qal & Hiph: rove, be restless

רוּחַ   to smell

רוּחַ   רוּחוֹת   spirit, breath, wind, f.

רוּץ   יָרוּץ   to run

רחב   be wide, spacious

רָחוֹק   adj. far, distant

רחץ   wash

רִיב   יָרִיב   to quarrel, argue

רֵיחַ   a scent, fragrance, m.

רֵיק   רֵיקָה   adj. empty, vain

רכב   Qal: to ride; Piel: to mount

רַע   רָעָה   adj. evil, bad

רֵעַ   a friend, a companion, m.

רעב   יִרְעַב   be hungry

רָעָב   a famine, m

רעה   feed, tend, shepherd

רֹעֶה   a shepherd, m.

רצח   יִרְצַח   to murder

רצץ   to bruise, crush

רַק   adv. only

שׂבע	יִשְׂבַּע	be satisfied, full
שָׂדֶה	שָׂדוֹת	a field, m.
שׂוּחַ		to meditate
שׂיב	שֵׂיבָה	grey hair, old age
שׂים		to place, put, set
שְׂמֹאל		left (hand)
שׂנא	יִשְׂנָא	to hate
שָׂעִיר		adj. hairy
שַׂר		a master, prince, chief, m.
שָׂרָה		Sarah

שׁאב	יִשְׁאַב	to draw (water)
שׁאה	יִשְׁאֶה	to gaze
שׁאל	יִשְׁאַל	to ask, inquire
שְׁאֹל		Sheol
שְׁאֵרִית		a remnant, f.
שׁבע	יִשָּׁבַע	to swear, take an oath
שֶׁבַע		seven, f.
שְׁבֻעָה		an oath, f.
שִׁבְעִים		seventy
שׁבר	יִשְׁבֹּר	to break; Piel: to shatter

214

שׁוּב	יָשׁוּב	to turn, return
שׁחה	יִשְׁתַּחֲוֶה	to bow down, prostrate oneself
שׁחט	יִשְׁחַט	to slay, slaughter
שָׁכַב	יִשְׁכַּב, שָׁכַב	to lie down
שׁכח	יִשְׁכַּח	to forget
שׁכל	יִשְׁכַּל	be bereaved (of children)
שׁכם		Hiph: get up early
שְׁכֶם		a shoulder, m.
שָׁכֵן	יִשְׁכֹּן, שָׁכַן	dwell, lie down
שׁלח	יִשְׁלַח	send forth
שֻׁלְחָן	שֻׁלְחָנוֹת	a table, m.
שְׁלֹמֹה		Solomon
שָׁם		adv. there
שֵׁם	שֵׁמוֹת	a name, m.
שָׁמַיִם		heavens
שֶׁמֶן		oil, fatness, fertility (of land), m.
שׁמע	יִשְׁמַע	hear
שׁמר	יִשְׁמֹר	watch, guard, keep
שְׁנַיִם		two, m, 5. Before a noun, שְׁנֵי
שַׁעַר	שְׁעָרִים	a gate, entrance, m.
שִׁפְחָה	שְׁפָחוֹת	a (female) slave, f.
שׁפט	יִשְׁפֹּט	to judge
שׁקה	יִשְׁקֶה	give a drink to
שׁקל	יִשְׁקֹל	weigh, pay
שׁקף		Niph & Hiph: look (at)
שֹׁקֶת		a watering-trough, f.

שִׁשָּׁה   six, m, 29; Fem: שֵׁשׁ; שִׁשִּׁים   sixty

שתה   יִשְׁתֶּה   drink

ת

תַּאֲוָה   a desire, wish, f.

תְּאוֹם   תְּאוֹמִים   a twin, m.

תאם   be double

תֶּבֶן   straw, m.

תּוֹלְדוֹת   generations, a history of (always plural)

תּוֹדָה   thanksgiving, f.

תָּוֶךְ   center, middle. Construct: תּוֹךְ

תּוֹרָה   Torah, law, instruction, f.

תַּחַת   under, instead of, in place of

תֵּימָן   South

תִּירוֹשׁ   new, unfermented wine, m.

תְּלִי   a quiver, m.

תַּלְמִיד   תַּלְמִידָה   a student, learner

תָּם   adj. complete, perfect

תעע   Pilpel: to sport, jest, mock

תִּקְוָה   hope, f.

VERB CHARTS APPENDIX

Pronominal Suffixes with the Verb

    Perfect
    Infinitive Construct
    Imperfect
    Imperative

Regular Verb - All Stems

Qal of Weak and Laryngael Verbs

Niphal of Weak and Laryngael Verbs

Hiphil of Weak and Laryngael Verbs

Hophal of Weak and Laryngael Verbs

Piel and Pual of Weak and Laryngael Verbs

Hitpael of Weak and Laryngael Verbs

Geminate or 'Ayin-Double Verbs

High-Frequency Pe-Nun Verbs

High-Frequency Hollow Verbs

High-Frequency Pe-Vav and Pe-Yod Verbs

Master Chart of Starter Forms of the Various
Classes of Hebrew Verbs

PRONOMINAL SUFFIXES WITH THE VERB*

THE PERFECT

	Singular					Plural		
	1st c.	2nd m.	2nd f.	3rd m.	3rd f.	1st c.	2nd m+f.	3rd c.
no suffix	שָׁמַרְתִּי	שָׁמַרְתָּ	שָׁמַרְתְּ	שָׁמַר	שָׁמְרָה	שָׁמַרְנוּ	שְׁמַרְתֶּם שְׁמַרְתֶּן	שָׁמְרוּ
sg. 1st c.		שְׁמַרְתַּנִי שְׁמַרְתָּנִי	שְׁמַרְתִּינִי	שְׁמָרַנִי	שְׁמָרַתְנִי		שְׁמַרְתּוּנִי	
2nd m.	שְׁמַרְתִּיךָ			שְׁמָרְךָ שְׁמָרֶךָ	שְׁמָרַתְךָ	שְׁמַרְנוּךָ		שְׁמָרוּךָ
2nd f.	שְׁמַרְתִּיךְ			שְׁמָרֵךְ	שְׁמָרַתֶךְ	שְׁמַרְנוּךְ		שְׁמָרוּךְ
3rd m.	שְׁמַרְתִּיהוּ שְׁמַרְתִּיו	שְׁמַרְתּוֹ שְׁמַרְתָּהוּ	שְׁמַרְתִּיהוּ	שְׁמָרוֹ שְׁמָרַתְהוּ שְׁמָרַתוּ	שְׁמָרַתְהוּ שְׁמָרָתוּ	שְׁמַרְנוּהוּ	שְׁמַרְתּוּהוּ	שְׁמָרוּהוּ
3rd f.	שְׁמַרְתִּיהָ	שְׁמַרְתָּהּ	שְׁמַרְתִּיהָ	שְׁמָרָהּ	שְׁמָרַתָּהּ	שְׁמַרְנוּהָ		שְׁמָרוּהָ
pl. 1st c.		שְׁמַרְתָּנוּ	שְׁמַרְתִּינוּ	שְׁמָרָנוּ	שְׁמָרַתְנוּ		שְׁמַרְתּוּנוּ	
2nd m.	שְׁמַרְתִּיכֶם					שמרנוכם		
2nd f.	שְׁמַרְתִּיכֶן							
3rd m.	שְׁמַרְתִּים	שְׁמַרְתָּם	שְׁמַרְתִּים	שְׁמָרָם	שְׁמָרַתָם	שְׁמָרָנוּם	שְׁמֵרְתּוּם	שְׁמָרוּם
3rd f.	שְׁמַרְתִּין	שְׁמַרְתָּן	שְׁמַרְתִּין	שְׁמָרָן	שְׁמָרַתָן		שְׁמַרְתּוּן	שְׁמָרוּן

THE INFINITIVE CONSTRUCT

	1st c.	2nd m.	2nd f.	3rd m.	3rd f.
sing.	שָׁמְרִי שָׁמְרֵנִי	שָׁמְרְךָ	שָׁמְרֵךְ	שָׁמְרוֹ	שָׁמְרָהּ
plural	שָׁמְרֵנוּ	שָׁמְרְכֶט	שָׁמְרְכֶן	שָׁמְרָם	שָׁמְרָן

* Only the Qal Stem is presented here. For more detailed information, see; Weingreen, pp. 123-135, or Lambdin, pp. 260-275.

THE IMPERFECT

	1st c.	2nd m. + 3rd f.	2nd f.	3rd m.	1st c.	2nd m.	3rd m.	2nd + 3rd f.
no suffix	אֶשְׁמֹר	תִּשְׁמֹר	תִּשְׁמְרִי	יִשְׁמֹר	נִשְׁמֹר	תִּשְׁמְרוּ	יִשְׁמְרוּ	תִּשְׁמֹרְנָה
sg. 1st c.		תִּשְׁמְרֵנִי / תִּשְׁמְרֵפִי		יִשְׁמְרֵנִי / יִשְׁמְרֵפִי		תִּשְׁמְרוּנִי	יִשְׁמְרוּנִי	
2nd m.	אֶשְׁמָרְךָ / אֶשְׁמְרֶךָ	תִּשְׁמָרְךָ / תִּשְׁמְרֶךָ		יִשְׁמָרְךָ / יִשְׁמְרֶךָ	נִשְׁמָרְךָ / נִשְׁמְרֶךָ		יִשְׁמְרוּךָ	
2nd f.	אֶשְׁמְרֵךְ	תִּשְׁמְרֵךְ		יִשְׁמְרֵךְ	נִשְׁמְרֵךְ		יִשְׁמְרוּךְ	
3rd m.	אֶשְׁמְרֵהוּ / אשמרנו	תִּשְׁמְרֵהוּ / תִּשְׁמְרֶנּוּ		יִשְׁמְרֵהוּ / יִשְׁמְרֶנּוּ	נִשְׁמְרֵהוּ / נִשְׁמְרֶנּוּ	תִּשְׁמְרוּהוּ	יִשְׁמְרוּהוּ	
3rd f.	אֶשְׁמְרֶהָ / אֶשְׁמְרֶנָּה	תִּשְׁמְרֶהָ / תִּשְׁמְרֶנָּה		יִשְׁמְרֶהָ / יִשְׁמְרֶנָּה	נִשְׁמְרֶהָ / נִשְׁמְרֶנָּה	תִּשְׁמְרוּהָ	יִשְׁמְרוּהָ	
pl. 1st c.	אֶשְׁמְרֵנוּ	תִּשְׁמְרֵנוּ		יִשְׁמְרֵנוּ		תִּשְׁמְרוּנוּ	יִשְׁמְרוּנוּ	
2nd m.	אֶשְׁמָרְכֶם	תִּשְׁמָרְכֶם		יִשְׁמָרְכֶם	נִשְׁמָרְכֶם		יִשְׁמְרוּכֶם	
2nd f.	אֶשְׁמָרְכֶן	תִּשְׁמָרְכֶן		יִשְׁמָרְכֶן	נִשְׁמָרְכֶן		יִשְׁמְרוּכֶן	
3rd m.	אֶשְׁמְרֵם	תִּשְׁמְרֵם		יִשְׁמְרֵם	נִשְׁמְרֵם	תִּשְׁמְרוּם	יִשְׁמְרוּם	
3rd f.	אֶשְׁמְרֵן	תִּשְׁמְרֵן		יִשְׁמְרֵן	נִשְׁמְרֵן	תִּשְׁמְרוּן	יִשְׁמְרוּן	

THE IMPERATIVE

The suffixes used are the same as those found in the Imperfect.
Therefore only these masculine examples are given.

	Singular 1st c.	3rd m.	3rd f.	Plural 1st c.	3rd m.	3rd f.
Masculine Singular	שָׁמְרֵנִי	שָׁמְרֵהוּ	שָׁמְרֶהָ	שָׁמְרֵנוּ	שָׁמְרֵם	שָׁמְרֵן
Masculine Plural	שִׁמְרוּנִי	שִׁמְרוּהוּ	שִׁמְרוּהָ	שִׁמְרוּנוּ	שִׁמְרוּם	שִׁמְרוּן

	Qal	Niphal	Piel	Pual	Hiphil	Hophal	Hitpael
pf. 1cs.	שָׁמַ֫רְתִּי	נִשְׁמַ֫רְתִּי	שִׁמַּ֫רְתִּי	שֻׁמַּ֫רְתִּי	הִשְׁבַּ֫רְתִּי	הָשְׁבַּ֫רְתִּי	הִשְׁתַּמַּ֫רְתִּי
2 m.	שָׁמַ֫רְתָּ	נִשְׁמַ֫רְתָּ	שִׁמַּ֫רְתָּ	שֻׁמַּ֫רְתָּ	הִשְׁבַּ֫רְתָּ	הָשְׁבַּ֫רְתָּ	הִשְׁתַּמַּ֫רְתָּ
2 f.	שָׁמַרְתְּ	נִשְׁמַרְתְּ	שִׁמַּרְתְּ	שֻׁמַּרְתְּ	הִשְׁבַּרְתְּ	הָשְׁבַּרְתְּ	הִשְׁתַּמַּרְתְּ
3 m.	שָׁמַר	נִשְׁמַר	שִׁמֵּר	שֻׁמַּר	הִשְׁבִּיר	הָשְׁבַּר	הִשְׁתַּמֵּר
3 f.	שָׁמְרָה	נִשְׁמְרָה	שִׁמְּרָה	שֻׁמְּרָה	הִשְׁבִּ֫ירָה	הָשְׁבְּרָה	הִשְׁתַּמְּרָה
1 c.p.	שָׁמַ֫רְנוּ	נִשְׁמַ֫רְנוּ	שִׁמַּ֫רְנוּ	שֻׁמַּ֫רְנוּ	הִשְׁבַּ֫רְנוּ	הָשְׁבַּ֫רְנוּ	הִשְׁתַּמַּ֫רְנוּ
2 m.	שְׁמַרְתֶּם	נִשְׁמַרְתֶּם	שִׁמַּרְתֶּם	שֻׁמַּרְתֶּם	הִשְׁבַּרְתֶּם	הָשְׁבַּרְתֶּם	הִשְׁתַּמַּרְתֶּם
2 f.	שְׁמַרְתֶּן	נִשְׁמַרְתֶּן	שִׁמַּרְתֶּן	שֻׁמַּרְתֶּן	הִשְׁבַּרְתֶּן	הָשְׁבַּרְתֶּן	הִשְׁתַּמַּרְתֶּן
3 c.	שָׁמְרוּ	נִשְׁמְרוּ	שִׁמְּרוּ	שֻׁמְּרוּ	הִשְׁבִּ֫ירוּ	הָשְׁבְּרוּ	הִשְׁתַּמְּרוּ
Imf. 1cs.	אֶשְׁמֹר	אֶשָּׁמֵר	אֲשַׁמֵּר	אֲשֻׁמַּר	אַשְׁבִּיר	אָשְׁבַּר	אֶשְׁתַּמֵּר
2m+3f	תִּשְׁמֹר	תִּשָּׁמֵר	תְּשַׁמֵּר	תְּשֻׁמַּר	תַּשְׁבִּיר	תָּשְׁבַּר	תִּשְׁתַּמֵּר
2 f.	תִּשְׁמְרִי	תִּשָּׁמְרִי	תְּשַׁמְּרִי	תְּשֻׁמְּרִי	תַּשְׁבִּ֫ירִי	תָּשְׁבְּרִי	תִּשְׁתַּמְּרִי
3 m.	יִשְׁמֹר	יִשָּׁמֵר	יְשַׁמֵּר	יְשֻׁמַּר	יַשְׁבִּיר	יָשְׁבַּר	יִשְׁתַּמֵּר
1 cp.	נִשְׁמֹר	נִשָּׁמֵר	נְשַׁמֵּר	נְשֻׁמַּר	נַשְׁבִּיר	נָשְׁבַּר	נִשְׁתַּמֵּר
2 m.	תִּשְׁמְרוּ	תִּשָּׁמְרוּ	תְּשַׁמְּרוּ	תְּשֻׁמְּרוּ	תַּשְׁבִּ֫ירוּ	תָּשְׁבְּרוּ	תִּשְׁתַּמְּרוּ
2f+3f	תִּשְׁמֹרְנָה	תִּשָּׁמַ֫רְנָה	תְּשַׁמֵּ֫רְנָה	תְּשֻׁמַּ֫רְנָה	תַּשְׁבֵּ֫רְנָה	תָּשְׁבַּ֫רְנָה	תִּשְׁתַּמֵּ֫רְנָה
3 m.	יִשְׁמְרוּ	יִשָּׁמְרוּ	יְשַׁמְּרוּ	יְשֻׁמְּרוּ	יַשְׁבִּ֫ירוּ	יָשְׁבְּרוּ	יִשְׁתַּמְּרוּ
Inf. C.	(לְ)שְׁמֹר	(לְ)הִשָּׁמֵר	(לְ)שַׁמֵּר	(לְ)שֻׁמַּר	(לְ)הַשְׁבִּיר	לְ הָשְׁבַּר	(לְ) הִשְׁתַּמֵּר
Inf. A.	שָׁמוֹר	נִשְׁמֹר (same or)	שַׁמֵּר	שֻׁמַּר	הַשְׁבֵּר	הָשְׁבֵּר	הִשְׁתַּמֵּר
Imv.s.m.	שְׁמֹר	הִשָּׁמֵר	שַׁמֵּר	שֻׁמַּר	הַשְׁבֵּר	does	הִשְׁתַּמֵּר
fem.	שִׁמְרִי	הִשָּׁמְרִי	שַׁמְּרִי	שֻׁמְּרִי	הַשְׁבִּ֫ירִי	not	הִשְׁתַּמְּרִי
pl m.	שִׁמְרוּ	הִשָּׁמְרוּ	שַׁמְּרוּ	שֻׁמְּרוּ	הַשְׁבִּ֫ירוּ	occur	הִשְׁתַּמְּרוּ
fem.	שְׁמֹרְנָה	הִשָּׁמַ֫רְנָה	שַׁמֵּ֫רְנָה	שֻׁמַּ֫רְנָה	הַשְׁבֵּ֫רְנָה		הִשְׁתַּמֵּ֫רְנָה
prt.s.m.	שֹׁמֵר	נִשְׁמָר	מְשַׁמֵּר	מְשֻׁמָּר	מַשְׁבִּיר	מָשְׁבָּר	מִשְׁתַּמֵּר
fem.	שֹׁמֶ֫רֶת	נִשְׁמָ֫רוּ	מְשַׁמֶּ֫רֶת	מְשֻׁמֶּ֫רֶת	מַשְׁבֶּ֫רֶת	מָשְׁבֶּ֫רֶת	מִשְׁתַּמֶּ֫רֶת
pl. m.	שֹׁמְרִים	נִשְׁמָרִים	מְשַׁמְּרִים	מְשֻׁמָּרִים	מַשְׁבִּירִים	מָשְׁבָּרִים	מִשְׁתַּמְּרִים
fem.	שֹׁמְרוֹת	נִשְׁמָרוֹת	מְשַׁמְּרוֹת	מְשֻׁמָּרוֹת	מַשְׁבִּירוֹת	מָשְׁבָּרוֹת	מִשְׁתַּמְּרוֹת
coh. s.	אֶשְׁמְרָה	אֶשָּׁמְרָה	אֲשַׁמְּרָה	אֲשֻׁמְּרָה	אַשְׁבִּ֫ירָה	אָשְׁבְּרָה	אֶשְׁתַּמְּרָה
coh. p.	נִשְׁמְרָה	נִשָּׁמְרָה	נְשַׁמְּרָה	נְשֻׁמְּרָה	נַשְׁבִּ֫ירָה	נָשְׁבְּרָה	נִשְׁתַּמְּרָה

	Hollow מת	PeʾPe ו ישב	Lamed-He שתה	Pe-Nun נגש	Pe-Aleph אכל	Pe-Lary עמד	ʿAyin-La שאל	Lam-Lary שלח	ʿAyin-D סבב
flcs.	מַתִּי	יָשַׁבְתִּי	שָׁתִיתִי	נָגַשְׁתִּי	אָכַלְתִּי	עָמַדְתִּי	שָׁאַלְתִּי	שָׁלַחְתִּי	סַבֹּתִי
m	מַתָּ	יָשַׁבְתָּ	שָׁתִיתָ	נָגַשְׁתָּ	אָכַלְתָּ	עָמַדְתָּ	שָׁאַלְתָּ	שָׁלַחְתָּ	סַבֹּתָ
f	מַתְּ	יָשַׁבְתְּ	שָׁתִית	נָגַשְׁתְּ	אָכַלְתְּ	עָמַדְתְּ	שָׁאַלְתְּ	שָׁלַחַתְּ	סַבֹּתְ
m	מֵת	יָשַׁב	שָׁתָה	נָגַשׁ	אָכַל	עָמַד	שָׁאַל	שָׁלַח	סָבַב
f	מֵתָה	יָשְׁבָה	שָׁתְתָה	נָגְשָׁה	אָכְלָה	עָמְדָה	שָׁאֲלָה	שָׁלְחָה	סָבְבָה
cpl	מַתְנוּ	יָשַׁבְנוּ	שָׁתִינוּ	נָגַשְׁנוּ	אָכַלְנוּ	עָמַדְנוּ	שָׁאַלְנוּ	שָׁלַחְנוּ	סַבּוֹנוּ
m	מַתֶּם	יְשַׁבְתֶּם	שְׁתִיתֶם	נְגַשְׁתֶּם	אֲכַלְתֶּם	עֲמַדְתֶּם	שְׁאַלְתֶּם	שְׁלַחְתֶּם	סַבֹּתֶם
f	מַתֶּן	יְשַׁבְתֶּן	שְׁתִיתֶן	נְגַשְׁתֶּן	אֲכַלְתֶּן	עֲמַדְתֶּן	שְׁאַלְתֶּן	שְׁלַחְתֶּן	סַבֹּתֶן
c	מֵתוּ	יָשְׁבוּ	שָׁתוּ	נָגְשׁוּ	אָכְלוּ	עָמְדוּ	שָׁאֲלוּ	שָׁלְחוּ	סָבְבוּ
mflcs	אָמוּת	אֵשֵׁב	אֶשְׁתֶּה	אֶגַּשׁ	אֹכַל	אֶעֱמֹד	אֶשְׁאַל	אֶשְׁלַח	אָסֹב
m+3f	תָּמוּת	תֵּשֵׁב	תִּשְׁתֶּה	תִּגַּשׁ	תֹּאכַל	תַּעֲמֹד	תִּשְׁאַל	תִּשְׁלַח	תָּסֹב
f	תָּמוּתִי	תֵּשְׁבִי	תִּשְׁתִּי	תִּגְּשִׁי	תֹּאכְלִי	תַּעַמְדִי	תִּשְׁאֲלִי	תִּשְׁלְחִי	תָּסֹבִּי
m	יָמוּת	יֵשֵׁב	יִשְׁתֶּה	יִגַּשׁ	יֹאכַל	יַעֲמֹד	יִשְׁאַל	יִשְׁלַח	יָסֹב
c.pl.	נָמוּת	נֵשֵׁב	נִשְׁתֶּה	נִגַּשׁ	נֹאכַל	נַעֲמֹד	נִשְׁאַל	נִשְׁלַח	נָסֹב
m	תָּמוּתוּ	תֵּשְׁבוּ	תִּשְׁתּוּ	תִּגְּשׁוּ	תֹּאכְלוּ	תַּעַמְדוּ	תִּשְׁאֲלוּ	תִּשְׁלְחוּ	תָּסֹבּוּ
f. + f.	תְּמוּתֶינָה, תְּמֻתֶנָה	תְּשַׁבְנָה	תִּשְׁתֶּינָה	תִּגַּשְׁנָה	תֹּאכַלְנָה	תַּעֲמֹדְנָה	תִּשְׁאַלְנָה	תִּשְׁלַחְנָה	תְּסֻבֶּינָה
m	יָמוּתוּ	יֵשְׁבוּ	יִשְׁתּוּ	יִגְּשׁוּ	יֹאכְלוּ	יַעַמְדוּ	יִשְׁאֲלוּ	יִשְׁלְחוּ	יָסֹבּוּ
nf C	(לָ)מוּת	(לָ)שֶׁבֶת	(לִ)שְׁתּוֹת	(לָ)גֶּשֶׁת	(לֶ)אֱכֹל	(לַ)עֲמֹד	(לִ)שְׁאֹל	(לִ)שְׁלֹחַ	סֹב
nf A	מוֹת	יָשׁוֹב	שָׁתֹה	נָגוֹשׁ	אָכֹל	עָמֹד	שָׁאֹל	שָׁלוֹחַ	סָבוֹב
mv.ms	מוּת	שֵׁב	שְׁתֵה	גַּשׁ	אֱכֹל	עֲמֹד	שְׁאַל	שְׁלַח	סֹב
. sg.	מוּתִי	שְׁבִי	שְׁתִי	גְּשִׁי	אִכְלִי	עִמְדִי	שַׁאֲלִי	שִׁלְחִי	סֹבִּי
. pl.	מוּתוּ	שְׁבוּ	שְׁתוּ	גְּשׁוּ	אִכְלוּ	עִמְדוּ	שַׁאֲלוּ	שִׁלְחוּ	סֹבּוּ
. pl.	מֹתְנָה	שֵׁבְנָה	שְׁתֶינָה	גֵּשְׁנָה	אֱכֹלְנָה	עֲמֹדְנָה	שְׁאַלְנָה	שְׁלַחְנָה	סֻבֶּינָה
rt.ms	מֵת	יוֹשֵׁב	שׁוֹתֶה	נֹגֵשׁ	אוֹכֵל	עוֹמֵד	שׁוֹאֵל	שׁוֹלֵחַ	סֹבֵב
. sg.	מֵתָה	יוֹשֶׁבֶת	שׁוֹתָה	נֹגֶשֶׁת	אוֹכֶלֶת	עוֹמֶדֶת	שׁוֹאֶלֶת	שׁוֹלַחַת	סֹבֶבֶת
. pl.	מֵתִים	יוֹשְׁבִים	שׁוֹתִים	נֹגְשִׁים	אוֹכְלִים	עוֹמְדִים	שׁוֹאֲלִים	שׁוֹלְחִים	סֹבְבִים
. pl.	מֵתוֹת	יוֹשְׁבוֹת	שׁוֹתוֹת	נֹגְשׁוֹת	אוֹכְלוֹת	עוֹמְדוֹת	שׁוֹאֲלוֹת	שׁוֹלְחוֹת	סֹבְבוֹת

	Hollow קום	Pe ‏י‎,Pe ‏ו‎ ישׁיב	Lamed-He גלה	Pe-Nun נגשׁ	Pe-Aleph אכל	Pe-Laryn עמד	Ayin-La שׁחט	Lamed-La שׁלח
Prflcs.	נְקוּמוֹתִי	נוֹשַׁבְתִּי	נִגְלֵיתִי	נִגַּשְׁתִּי	נֶאֱכַלְתִּי	נֶעֱמַדְתִּי	נִשְׁחַטְתִּי	נִשְׁלַחְתִּי
2m	נְקוּמוֹתָ	נוֹשַׁבְתָּ	נִגְלֵיתָ	נִגַּשְׁתָּ	נֶאֱכַלְתָּ	נֶעֱמַדְתָּ	נִשְׁחַטְתָּ	נִשְׁלַחְתָּ
2f	נְקוּמוֹתְ	נוֹשַׁבְתְּ	נִגְלֵיתְ	נִגַּשְׁתְּ	נֶאֱכַלְתְּ	נֶעֱמַדְתְּ	נִשְׁחַטְתְּ	נִשְׁלַחְתְּ
3m	נָקוֹם	נוֹשַׁב	נִגְלָה	נִגַּשׁ	נֶאֱכַל	נֶעֱמַד	נִשְׁחַט	נִשְׁלַח
3f	נָקוֹמָה	נוֹשְׁבָה	נִגְלְתָה	נִגְּשָׁה	נֶאֶכְלָה	נֶעֶמְדָה	נִשְׁחֲטָה	נִשְׁלְחָה
1cpl	נְקוּמוֹנוּ	נוֹשַׁבְנוּ	נִגְלֵינוּ	נִגַּשְׁנוּ	נֶאֱכַלְנוּ	נֶעֱמַדְנוּ	נִשְׁחַטְנוּ	נִשְׁלַחְנוּ
2m	נְקוּמוֹתֶם	נוֹשַׁבְתֶּם	נִגְלֵיתֶם	נִגַּשְׁתֶּם	נֶאֱכַלְתֶּם	נֶעֱמַדְתֶּם	נִשְׁחַטְתֶּם	נִשְׁלַחְתֶּם
2f	נְקוּמוֹתֶן	נוֹשַׁבְתֶּן	נִגְלֵיתֶן	נִגַּשְׁתֶּן	נֶאֱכַלְתֶּן	נֶעֱמַדְתֶּן	נִשְׁחַטְתֶּן	נִשְׁלַחְתֶּן
3c	נָקוֹמוּ	נוֹשְׁבוּ	נִגְלוּ	נִגְּשׁוּ	נֶאֶכְלוּ	נֶעֶמְדוּ	נִשְׁחֲטוּ	נִשְׁלְחוּ
Imflcs.	אֶקּוֹם	אִוָּשֵׁב	אֶגָּלֶה	אֶנָּגֵשׁ	אֵאָכֵל	אֵעָמֵד	אֶשָּׁחֵט	אֶשָּׁלַח
2m+3f	תִּקּוֹם	תִּוָּשֵׁב	תִּגָּלֶה	תִּנָּגֵשׁ	תֵּאָכֵל	תֵּעָמֵד	תִּשָּׁחֵט	תִּשָּׁלַח
2f	תִּקּוֹמִי	תִּוָּשְׁבִי	תִּגָּלִי	תִּנָּגְשִׁי	תֵּאָכְלִי	תֵּעָמְדִי	תִּשָּׁחֲטִי	תִּשָּׁלְחִי
3m	יִקּוֹם	יִוָּשֵׁב	יִגָּלֶה	יִנָּגֵשׁ	יֵאָכֵל	יֵעָמֵד	יִשָּׁחֵט	יִשָּׁלַח
1cpl.	נִקּוֹם	נִוָּשֵׁב	נִגָּלֶה	נִנָּגֵשׁ	נֵאָכֵל	נֵעָמֵד	נִשָּׁחֵט	נִשָּׁלַח
2m	תִּקּוֹמוּ	תִּוָּשְׁבוּ	תִּגָּלוּ	תִּנָּגְשׁוּ	תֵּאָכְלוּ	תֵּעָמְדוּ	תִּשָּׁחֲטוּ	תִּשָּׁלְהוּ
2f+3f	תִּקּוֹמְנָה	תִּוָּשַׁבְנָה	תִּגָּלֶינָה	תִּנָּגַשְׁנָה	תֵּאָכַלְנָה	תֵּעָמַדְנָה	תִּשָּׁחַטְנָה	תִּשָּׁלַחְנָה
3m	יִקּוֹמוּ	יִוָּשְׁבוּ	יִגָּלוּ	יִנָּגְשׁוּ	יֵאָכְלוּ	יֵעָמְדוּ	יִשָּׁחֲטוּ	יִשָּׁלְחוּ
Inf C	(לְ)הִקּוֹם	(לְ)הִוָּשֵׁב	הִגָּלוֹת	הִנָּגֵשׁ	(לְ)הֵאָכֵל	(לְ)הֵעָמֵד	הִשָּׁחֵט	(לְ)הִשָּׁלַח
Inf A	הִקּוֹם	הִוָּשֵׁב	נִגְלֹה	הִנָּגֹשׁ	הֵאָכֹל	הֵעָמֹד	נִשָּׁחוֹט	הִשָּׁלֹחַ
Imv.ms.	הִקּוֹם	הִוָּשֵׁב	הִגָּלֵה	הִנָּגֵשׁ	הֵאָכֵל	הֵעָמֵד	הִשָּׁחֵט	הִשָּׁלַח
f. sg.	הִקּוֹמִי	הִוָּשְׁבִי	הִגָּלִי	הִנָּגְשִׁי	הֵאָכְלִי	הֵעָמְדִי	הִשָּׁחֲטִי	הִשָּׁלְחִי
m. pl.	הִקּוֹמוּ	הִוָּשְׁבוּ	הִגָּלוּ	הִנָּגְשׁוּ	הֵאָכְלוּ	הֵעָמְדוּ	הִשָּׁחֲטוּ	הִשָּׁלְחוּ
f. pl.	הִקּוֹמְנָה	הִוָּשַׁבְנָה	הִגָּלֶינָה	הִנָּגַשְׁנָה	הֵאָכַלְנָה	הֵעָמַדְנָה	הִשָּׁחַטְנָה	הִשָּׁלַחְנָה
Prt. ms.	נָקוֹם	נוֹשָׁב	נִגְלֶה	נִגָּשׁ	נֶאֱכָל	נֶעֱמָד	נִשְׁחָט	נִשְׁלָח
f. sg.	נְקוֹמָה	נוֹשֶׁבֶת	נִגְלָה	נִגֶּשֶׁת	נֶאֱכֶלֶת	נֶעֱמָדָה	נִשְׁחָטָה	נִשְׁלַחַת
m. pl.	נְקוֹמִים	נוֹשָׁבִים	נִגְלִים	נִגָּשִׁים	נֶאֱכָלִים	נֶעֱמָדִים	נִשְׁחָטִים	נִשְׁלָחִים
f. pl.	נְקוֹמוֹת	נוֹשָׁבוֹת	נִגְלוֹת	נִגָּשׁוֹת	נֶאֱכָלוֹת	נֶעֱמָדוֹת	נִשְׁחָטוֹת	נִשְׁלָחוֹת

HIPHIL OF WEAK AND LARINGAEL VERBS

	Hollow קוט	Pe' Pe ישב	Lamedh-He גלה	Pe-Nun נגש	Pe-Aleph אכל	Pe-Lary עמד	Ayin-La. שאל	Lamedh Laryn שלה
Prf.1cs.	הֲקִימוֹתִי	הוֹשַׁבְתִּי	הִגְלֵיתִי	הִגַּשְׁתִּי	הֶאֱכַלְתִּי	הֶעֱמַדְתִּי	הִשְׁאַלְתִּי	הִשְׁלַהְתִּי
2m	הֲקִימוֹתָ	הוֹשַׁבְתָּ	הִגְלֵיתָ	הִגַּשְׁתָּ	הֶאֱכַלְתָּ	הֶעֱמַדְתָּ	הִשְׁאַלְתָּ	הִשְׁלַהְתָּ
2f	הֲקִימוֹת	הוֹשַׁבְתְּ	הִגְלֵית	הִגַּשְׁתְּ	הֶאֱכַלְתְּ	הֶעֱמַדְתְּ	הִשְׁאַלְתְּ	הִשְׁלַהַתְּ
3m	הֵקִים	הוֹשִׁיב	הִגְלָה	הִגִּישׁ	הֶאֱכִיל	הֶעֱמִיד	הִשְׁאִיל	הִשְׁלִיחַ
3f	הֵקִימָה	הוֹשִׁיבָה	הִגְלְתָה	הִגִּישָׁה	הֶאֱכִילָה	הֶעֱמִידָה	הִשְׁאִילָה	הִשְׁלִיחָה
1cpl.	הֲקִימוֹנוּ	הוֹשַׁבְנוּ	הִגְלֵינוּ	הִגַּשְׁנוּ	הֶאֱכַלְנוּ	הֶעֱמַדְנוּ	הִשְׁאַלְנוּ	הִשְׁלַהְנוּ
2m	הֲקִימוֹתֶם	הוֹשַׁבְתֶּם	הִגְלֵיתֶם	הִגַּשְׁתֶּם	הֶאֱכַלְתֶּם	הֶעֱמַדְתֶּם	הִשְׁאַלְתֶּם	הִשְׁלַהְתֶּם
2f	הֲקִימוֹתֶן	הוֹשַׁבְתֶּן	הִגְלֵיתֶן	הִגַּשְׁתֶּן	הֶאֱכַלְתֶּן	הֶעֱמַדְתֶּן	הִשְׁאַלְתֶּן	הִשְׁלַהְתֶּן
3c	הֵקִימוּ	הוֹשִׁיבוּ	הִגְלוּ	הִגִּישׁוּ	הֶאֱכִילוּ	הֶעֱמִידוּ	הִשְׁאִילוּ	הִשְׁלִיהוּ
Imf.1cs.	אָקִים	אוֹשִׁיב	אַגְלֶה	אַגִּישׁ	אַאֲכִיל	אַעֲמִיד	אַשְׁאִיל	אַשְׁלִיהַ
2m+3f	תָּקִים	תּוֹשִׁיב	תַּגְלֶה	תַּגִּישׁ	תַּאֲכִיל	תַּעֲמִיד	תַּשְׁאִיל	תַּשְׁלִיהַ
2f	תָּקִימִי	תּוֹשִׁיבִי	תַּגְלִי	תַּגִּישִׁי	תַּאֲכִילִי	תַּעֲמִידִי	תַּשְׁאִילִי	תַּשְׁלִיחִי
3m	יָקִים	יוֹשִׁיב	יַגְלֶה	יַגִּישׁ	יַאֲכִיל	יַעֲמִיד	יַשְׁאִיל	יַשְׁלִיחַ
1cpl.	נָקִים	נוֹשִׁיב	נַגְלֶה	נַגִּישׁ	נַאֲכִיל	נַעֲמִיד	נַשְׁאִיל	נַשְׁלִיחַ
2m	תָּקִימוּ	תּוֹשִׁיבוּ	תַּגְלוּ	תַּגִּישׁוּ	תַּאֲכִילוּ	תַּעֲמִידוּ	תַּשְׁאִילוּ	תַּשְׁלִיהוּ
2f. + 3f.	תָּקֹמְנָה or תְּקִימֶינָה	תּוֹשֵׁבְנָה	תַּגְלֶינָה	תַּגֵּשְׁנָה	תַּאֲכֵלְנָה	תַּעֲמֵדְנָה	תַּשְׁאֵלְנָה	תַּשְׁלַחְנָה
3m	יָקִימוּ	יוֹשִׁיבוּ	יַגְלוּ	יַגִּישׁוּ	יַאֲכִילוּ	יַעֲמִידוּ	יַשְׁאִילוּ	יַשְׁלִיהוּ
Inf C.	(לְ)הָקִים	(לְ)הוֹשִׁיב	(לְ)הַגְלוֹת	(לְ)הַגִּישׁ	(לְ)הַאֲכִיל	(לְ)הַעֲמִיד	(לְ)הַשְׁאִיל	(לְ)הַשְׁלִיחַ
Inf A.	הָקֵם	הוֹשֵׁב	הַגְלֵה	הַגֵּשׁ	הַאֲכֵל	הַעֲמֵד	הַשְׁאֵל	הַשְׁלֵחַ
Imv.ms.	הָקֵם	הוֹשֵׁב	הַגְלֵה	הַגֵּשׁ	הַאֲכֵל	הַעֲמֵד	הַשְׁאֵל	הַשְׁלַח
f. sg.	הָקִימִי	הוֹשִׁיבִי	הַגְלִי	הַגִּישִׁי	הַאֲכִילִי	הַעֲמִידִי	הַשְׁאִילִי	הַשְׁלִיחִי
m. pl.	הָקִימוּ	הוֹשִׁיבוּ	הַגְלוּ	הַגִּישׁוּ	הַאֲכִילוּ	הַעֲמִידוּ	הַשְׁאִילוּ	הַשְׁלִיהוּ
f. pl.	הָקֵמְנָה	הוֹשֵׁבְנָה	הַגְלֶינָה	הַגֵּשְׁנָה	הַאֲכֵלְנָה	הַעֲמֵדְנָה	הַשְׁאֵלְנָה	הַשְׁלַחְנָה
Prt.ms.	מֵקִים	מוֹשִׁיב	מַגְלֶה	מַגִּישׁ	מַאֲכִיל	מַעֲמִיד	מַשְׁאִיל	מַשְׁלִיחַ
f. sg.	מְקִימָה	מוֹשֶׁבֶת	מַגְלָה	מַגֶּשֶׁת	מַאֲכִלָה	מַעֲמֶדֶת	מַשְׁאֶלֶת	מַשְׁלַחַת
m. pl.	מְקִימִים	מוֹשִׁיבִים	מַגְלִים	מַגִּישִׁים	מַאֲכִילִים	מַעֲמִידִים	מַשְׁאִילִים	מַשְׁלִיהִים
f. pl.	מְקִימוֹת	מוֹשִׁיבוֹת	מַגְלוֹת	מַגִּישׁוֹת	מַאֲכִילוֹת	מַעֲמִידוֹת	מַשְׁאִילוֹת	מַשְׁלִיהוֹת

	Hollow קום	Pe י Pe ן ישב	Lam.-He גלה	Pe-Nun נגש	Pe-Aleph אכל	Pe-Lary. עמד	ʿAyin Laryng. שאל	Lamedh Laryng. שלח
Prf.1cs.	הוּקַמְתִּי	הוּשַׁבְתִּי	הָגְלֵיתִי	הֻגַּשְׁתִּי	הָאֳכַלְתִּי	הָעֳמַדְתִּי	הָשְׁאַלְתִּי	הָשְׁלַהְתִּי
2m	הוּקַמְתָּ	הוּשַׁבְתָּ	הָגְלֵיתָ	הֻגַּשְׁתָּ	הָאֳכַלְתָּ	הָעֳמַדְתָּ	הָשְׁאַלְתָּ	הָשְׁלַהְתָּ
2f	הוּקַמְתְּ	הוּשַׁבְתְּ	הָגְלֵיתְ	הֻגַּשְׁתְּ	הָאֳכַלְתְּ	הָעֳמַדְתְּ	הָשְׁאַלְתְּ	הָשְׁלַהְתְּ
3m	הוּקַם	הוּשַׁב	הָגְלָה	הֻגַּשׁ	הָאֳכַל	הָעֳמַד	הָשְׁאַל	הָשְׁלַח
3f	הוּקְמָה	הוּשְׁבָה	הָגְלְתָה	הֻגְּשָׁה	הָאֳכְלָה	הָעֳמְדָה	הָשְׁאֲלָה	הָשְׁלְהָה
1 c. p.	הוּקַמְנוּ	הוּשַׁבְנוּ	הָגְלֵינוּ	הֻגַּשְׁנוּ	הָאֳכַלְנוּ	הָעֳמַדְנוּ	הָשְׁאַלְנוּ	הָשְׁלַהְנוּ
2m	הוּקַמְתֶּם	הוּשַׁבְתֶּם	הָגְלֵיתֶם	הֻגַּשְׁתֶּם	הָאֳכַלְתֶּם	הָעֳמַדְתֶּם	הָשְׁאַלְתֶּם	הָשְׁלַהְתֶּם
2f	הוּקַמְתֶּן	הוּשַׁבְתֶּן	הָגְלֵיתֶן	הֻגַּשְׁתֶּן	הָאֳכַלְתֶּן	הָעֳמַדְתֶּן	הָשְׁאַלְתֶּן	הָשְׁלַחְתֶּן
3c	הוּקְמוּ	הוּשְׁבוּ	הָגְלוּ	הֻגְּשׁוּ	הָאֳכְלוּ	הָעֳמְדוּ	הָשְׁאֲלוּ	הָשְׁלְהוּ
Imf.1cs.	אוּקַם	אוּשַׁב	אָגְלֶה	אֻגַּשׁ	אָאֳכַל	אָעֳמַד	אָשְׁאַל	אָשְׁלַה
2m+3f	תּוּקַם	תּוּשַׁב	תָּגְלֶה	תֻּגַּשׁ	תָּאֳכַל	תָּעֳמַד	תָּשְׁאַל	תָּשְׁלַה
2f	תּוּקְמִי	תּוּשְׁבִי	תָּגְלִי	תֻּגְּשִׁי	תָּאֳכְלִי	תָּעֳמְדִי	תָּשְׁאֲלִי	תָּשְׁלְהִי
3m	יוּקַם	יוּשַׁב	יָגְלֶה	יֻגַּשׁ	יָאֳכַל	יָעֳמַד	יָשְׁאַל	יָשְׁלַה
1 c. p.	נוּקַם	נוּשַׁב	נָגְלֶה	נֻגַּשׁ	נָאֳכַל	נָעֳמַד	נָשְׁאַל	נָשְׁלַה
2m	תּוּקְמוּ	תּוּשְׁבוּ	תָּגְלוּ	תֻּגְּשׁוּ	תָּאֳכְלוּ	תָּעֳמְדוּ	תָּשְׁאֲלוּ	תָּשְׁלְהוּ
2f+3f	תּוּקַמְנָה	תּוּשַׁבְנָה	תָּגְלֶינָה	תֻּגַּשְׁנָה	תָּאֳכַלְנָה	תָּעֳמַדְנָה	תָּשְׁאַלְנָה	תָּשְׁלַהְנָה
3m	יוּקְמוּ	יוּשְׁבוּ	יָגְלוּ	יֻגְּשׁוּ	יָאֳכְלוּ	יָעֳמְדוּ	יָשְׁאֲלוּ	יָשְׁלְהוּ
Inf C.	הוּקַם	(לְ)הוּשַׁב	הָגְלוֹת		הָאֳכַל	הָעֳמַד		
Inf A.	הוּקַם	הוּשֵׁב	הָגְלֵה	הֻגֵּשׁ	הָאֳכֵל	הָעֳמֵד	הָשְׁאֵל	הָשְׁלֵהַ
Imv. ms.	Does	Does	Does	Does	Does	Does	Does	Does
f. sg.	not	not	not	not	not	not	not	not
m. pl.	Occur	Occur	Occur	Occur	Occur	Occur	Occur	Occur
f. pl.								
Prt. ms.	מוּקָם	מוּשָׁב	מָגְלֶה	מֻגָּשׁ	מָאֳכָל	מָעֳמָד	מָשְׁאָל	מָשְׁלֶה
f. sg.	מוּקֶמֶת	מוּשֶׁבֶת	מָגְלָה	מֻגֶּשֶׁת	מָאֳכֶלֶת	מָעֳמֶדֶת	מָשְׁאֶלֶת	מָשְׁלַהַת
m. pl.	מוּקָמִים	מוּשָׁבִים	מָגְלִיט	מֻגָּשִׁים	מָאֳכָלִים	מָעֳמָדִיט	מָשְׁאָלִים	מָשְׁלָהִיט
f. pl.	מוּקָמוֹת	מוּשָׁבוֹת	מָגְלוֹת	מֻגָּשׁוֹת	מָאֳכָלוֹת	מָעֳמָדוֹת	מָשְׁאָלוֹת	מָשְׁלָהוֹת

	Hollow Polel קום	Hollow Polal קום	Lam.-He Piel גלה	Lam.-He Pual גלה	'AyinLa. Piel ברך	AyinLa. Pual ברך	Lam.Lar. Piel שלח	Lam.Lar. Pual שלח
Prf.1cs.	קוֹמַמְתִּי	קוֹמַמְתִּי	גִּלִּיתִי	גֻּלֵּיתִי	בֵּרַכְתִּי	בֹּרַכְתִּי	שִׁלַּחְתִּי	שֻׁלַּחְתִּי
2m	קוֹמַמְתָּ	קוֹמַמְתָּ	גִּלִּיתָ	גֻּלֵּיתָ	בֵּרַכְתָּ	בֹּרַכְתָּ	שִׁלַּחְתָּ	שֻׁלַּחְתָּ
2f	קוֹמַמְתְּ	קוֹמַמְתְּ	גִּלִּיתְ	גֻּלֵּיתְ	בֵּרַכְתְּ	בֹּרַכְתְּ	שִׁלַּחַתְּ	שֻׁלַּחַתְּ
3m	קוֹמֵם	קוֹמַם	גִּלָּה	גֻּלָּה	בֵּרַךְ	בֹּרַךְ	שִׁלַּח	שֻׁלַּח
3f	קוֹמְמָה	קוֹמְמָה	גִּלְּתָה	גֻּלְּתָה	בֵּרְכָה	בֹּרְכָה	שִׁלְּחָה	שֻׁלְּחָה
1 c. p.	קוֹמַמְנוּ	קוֹמַמְנוּ	גִּלִּינוּ	גֻּלֵּינוּ	בֵּרַכְנוּ	בֹּרַכְנוּ	שִׁלַּחְנוּ	שֻׁלַּחְנוּ
2m	קוֹמַמְתֶּם	קוֹמַמְתֶּם	גִּלִּיתֶם	גֻּלֵּיתֶם	בֵּרַכְתֶּם	בֹּרַכְתֶּם	שִׁלַּחְתֶּם	שֻׁלַּחְתֶּם
2f	קוֹמַמְתֶּן	קוֹמַמְתֶּן	גִּלִּיתֶן	גֻּלֵּיתֶן	בֵּרַכְתֶּן	בֹּרַכְתֶּן	שִׁלַּחְתֶּן	שֻׁלַּחְתֶּן
3c	קוֹמְמוּ	קוֹמְמוּ	גִּלּוּ	גֻּלּוּ	בֵּרְכוּ	בֹּרְכוּ	שִׁלְּחוּ	שֻׁלְּחוּ
Imf.1cs.	אֲקוֹמֵם	אֲקוֹמַם	אֲגַלֶּה	אֲגֻלֶּה	אֲבָרֵךְ	אֲבֹרַךְ	אֲשַׁלַּח	אֲשֻׁלַּח
2m+3f	תְּקוֹמֵם	תְּקוֹמַם	תְּגַלֶּה	תְּגֻלֶּה	תְּבָרֵךְ	תְּבֹרַךְ	תְּשַׁלַּח	תְּשֻׁלַּח
2f	תְּקוֹמְמִי	תְּקוֹמְמִי	תְּגַלִּי	תְּגֻלִּי	תְּבָרְכִי	תְּבֹרְכִי	תְּשַׁלְּחִי	תְּשֻׁלְּחִי
3m	יְקוֹמֵם	יְקוֹמַם	יְגַלֶּה	יְגֻלֶּה	יְבָרֵךְ	יְבֹרַךְ	יְשַׁלַּח	יְשֻׁלַּח
1 c. p.	נְקוֹמֵם	נְקוֹמַם	נְגַלֶּה	נְגֻלֶּה	נְבָרֵךְ	נְבֹרַךְ	נְשַׁלַּח	נְשֻׁלַּח
2m	תְּקוֹמְמוּ	תְּקוֹמְמוּ	תְּגַלּוּ	תְּגֻלּוּ	תְּבָרְכוּ	תְּבֹרְכוּ	תְּשַׁלְּחוּ	תְּשֻׁלְּחוּ
2f+3f	תְּקוֹמֵמְנָה	תְּקוֹמַמְנָה	תְּגַלֶּינָה	תְּגֻלֶּינָה	תְּבָרֵכְנָה	תְּבֹרַכְנָה	תְּשַׁלַּחְנָה	תְּשֻׁלַּחְנָה
3m	יְקוֹמְמוּ	יְקוֹמְמוּ	יְגַלּוּ	יְגֻלּוּ	יְבָרְכוּ	יְבֹרְכוּ	יְשַׁלְּחוּ	יְשֻׁלְּחוּ
Inf C.	קוֹמֵם		גַּלּוֹת	גֻּלּוֹת	(לְ)בָרֵךְ		(לְ)שַׁלֵּחַ	
Inf A.	קוֹמֵם	קוֹמֵם	גַּלֵּה	גֻּלֵּה	בָּרֵךְ	בֹּרֵךְ	שַׁלֵּחַ	שֻׁלֵּחַ
Imv.ms.	קוֹמֵם	Does	גַּלֵּה	Does	בָּרֵךְ	Does	שַׁלַּח	Does
f. sg.	קוֹמְמִי	Not	גַּלִּי	Not	בָּרְכִי	Not	שַׁלְּחִי	Not
m. pl.	קוֹמְמוּ	Occur	גַּלּוּ	Occur	בָּרְכוּ	Occur	שַׁלְּחוּ	Occur
f. pl.	קוֹמֵמְנָה		גַּלֶּינָה		בָּרֵכְנָה		שַׁלַּחְנָה	
Prt.m s.	מְקוֹמֵם	מְקוֹמָם	מְגַלֶּה	מְגֻלֶּה	מְבָרֵךְ	מְבֹרָךְ	מְשַׁלֵּחַ	מְשֻׁלָּח
f. sg.	מְקוֹמֶמֶת	מְקוֹמֶמֶת	מְגַלָּה	מְגֻלָּה	מְבָרֶכֶת	מְבֹרֶכֶת	מְשַׁלַּחַת	מְשֻׁלַּחַת
m. pl.	מְקוֹמְמִים	מְקוֹמָמִים	מְגַלִּים	מְגֻלִּים	מְבָרְכִים	מְבֹרָכִים	מְשַׁלְּחִים	מְשֻׁלָּחִים
f. pl.	מְקוֹמְמוֹת	מְקוֹמָמוֹת	מְגַלּוֹת	מְגֻלּוֹת	מְבָרְכוֹת	מְבֹרָכוֹת	מְשַׁלְּחוֹת	מְשֻׁלָּחוֹת

HITPAEL OF WEAK AND LARYNGAEL VERBS

	Hollow קום	Pe-י Pe-ו ידע	'Ayin-Lary. ברך	Lam.-Laryng. שלח
Prf. 1cs.	הִתְקוֹמַמְתִּי	הִתְוַדַּעְתִּי	הִתְבָּרַכְתִּי	הִשְׁתַּלַּחְתִּי
2. m.	הִתְקוֹמַמְתָּ	הִתְוַדַּעְתָּ	הִתְבָּרַכְתָּ	הִשְׁתַּלַּחְתָּ
2. f.	הִתְקוֹמַמְתְּ	הִתְוַדַּעְתְּ	הִתְבָּרַכְתְּ	הִשְׁתַּלַּחְתְּ
3. m.	הִתְקוֹמֵם	הִתְוַדַּע	הִתְבָּרַךְ	הִשְׁתַּלַּח
3. f.	הִתְקוֹמְמָה	הִתְוַדְּעָה	הִתְבָּרְכָה	הִשְׁתַּלְּחָה
1 c. p.	הִתְקוֹמַמְנוּ	הִתְוַדַּעְנוּ	הִתְבָּרַכְנוּ	הִשְׁתַּלַּחְנוּ
2. m.	הִתְקוֹמַמְתֶּם	הִתְוַדַּעְתֶּם	הִתְבָּרַכְתֶּם	הִשְׁתַּלַּחְתֶּם
2. f.	הִתְקוֹמַמְתֶּן	הִתְוַדַּעְתֶּן	הִתְבָּרַכְתֶּן	הִשְׁתַּלַּחְתֶּן
3. c.	הִתְקוֹמְמוּ	הִתְוַדְּעוּ	הִתְבָּרְכוּ	הִשְׁתַּלְּחוּ
Imf. 1cs.	אֶתְקוֹמֵם	אֶתְוַדַּע	אֶתְבָּרֵךְ	אֶשְׁתַּלָּה
2m + 3f	תִּתְקוֹמֵם	תִּתְוַדַּע	תִּתְבָּרֵךְ	תִּשְׁתַּלָּה
2. f.	תִּתְקוֹמְמִי	תִּתְוַדְּעִי	תִּתְבָּרְכִי	תִּשְׁתַּלְּהִי
3. m.	יִתְקוֹמֵם	יִתְוַדַּע	יִתְבָּרֵךְ	יִשְׁתַּלַּה
1 c. p.	נִתְקוֹמֵם	נִתְוַדַּע	נִתְבָּרֵךְ	נִשְׁתַּלַּה
2. m.	תִּתְקוֹמְמוּ	תִּתְוַדְּעוּ	תִּתְבָּרְכוּ	תִּשְׁתַּלְּהוּ
2f + 3f	תִּתְקוֹמֵמְנָה	תִּתְוַדַּעְנָה	תִּתְבָּרֵכְנָה	תִּשְׁתַּלַּהְנָה
3. m.	יִתְקוֹמְמוּ	יִתְוַדְּעוּ	יִתְבָּרְכוּ	יִשְׁתַּלְּהוּ
Inf C.	(לְ)הִתְקוֹמֵם	(לְ)הִתְוַדַּע	(לְ)הִתְבָּרֵךְ	(לְ)הִשְׁתַּלַּח
Inf A.	הִתְקוֹמֵם	הִתְוַדֵּעַ	הִתְבָּרֵךְ	הִשְׁתַּלֵּחַ
Imv. m.s.	הִתְקוֹמֵם	הִתְוַדַּע	הִתְבָּרֵךְ	הִשְׁתַּלַּח
fem. sg.	הִתְקוֹמְמִי	הִתְוַדְּעִי	הִתְבָּרְכִי	הִשְׁתַּלְּהִי
masc. pl.	הִתְקוֹמְמוּ	הִתְוַדְּעוּ	הִתְבָּרְכוּ	הִשְׁתַּלְּהוּ
fem. pl.	הִתְקוֹמֵמְנָה	הִתְוַדַּעְנָה	הִתְבָּרֵכְנָה	הִשְׁתַּלַּהְנָה
Prt. ms.	מִתְקוֹמֵם	מִתְוַדֵּעַ	מִתְבָּרֵךְ	מִשְׁתַּלֵּהַ
fem. sg.	מִתְקוֹמֶמֶת	מִתְוַדַּעַת	מִתְבָּרֶכֶת	מִשְׁתַּלַּהַת
masc. pl.	מִתְקוֹמְמִים	מִתְוַדְּעִים	מִתְבָּרְכִים	מִשְׁתַּלְּהִים
fem. pl.	מִתְקוֹמְמוֹת	מִתְוַדְּעוֹת	מִתְבָּרְכוֹת	מִשְׁתַּלְּהוֹת

	QAL	Qal(alt)	Niphal	Poel	Poal	Hiphil	Hophal	Hitpael
Prf.1cs.	סַבֹּ֫תִי	סַבּ֫וֹתִי	נְסַבּ֫וֹתִי	סוֹבַ֫בְתִּי	סוֹבַ֫בְתִּי	הֲסִבּ֫וֹתִי	הוּסַבּ֫וֹתִי	הִסְתּוֹבַ֫בְתִּי
2m	סַבֹּ֫תָ	סַבּ֫וֹתָ	נְסַבּ֫וֹתָ	סוֹבַ֫בְתָּ	סוֹבַ֫בְתָּ	הֲסִבּ֫וֹתָ	הוּסַבּ֫וֹתָ	הִסְתּוֹבַ֫בְתָּ
2f	סַבֹּ֫ת	סַבּ֫וֹת	נְסַבּ֫וֹת	סוֹבַ֫בְתְּ	סוֹבַ֫בְתְּ	הֲסִבּ֫וֹת	הוּסַבּ֫וֹת	הִסְתּוֹבַ֫בְתְּ
3m	סָבַב	סַב	נָסַב	סוֹבֵב	סוֹבַב	הֵסֵב	הוּסַב	הִסְתּוֹבֵב
3f	סָֽבְבָה	סַ֫בָּה	נָסַ֫בָּה	סוֹבְבָה	סוֹבְבָה	הֵסֵ֫בָּה	הוּסַ֫בָּה	הִסְתּוֹבְבָה
1 c. p.	סַבֹּ֫נוּ	סַבּ֫וֹנוּ	נְסַבּ֫וֹנוּ	סוֹבַ֫בְנוּ	סוֹבַ֫בְנוּ	הֲסִבּ֫וֹנוּ	הוּסַבּ֫וֹנוּ	הִסְתּוֹבַ֫בְנוּ
2m	סַבֹּתֶם	סַבּוֹתֶם	נְסַבּוֹתֶם	סוֹבַבְתֶּם	סוֹבַבְתֶּם	הֲסִבּוֹתֶם	הוּסַבּוֹתֶם	הִסְתּוֹבַבְתֶּם
2f	סַבֹּתֶן	סַבּוֹתֶן	נְסַבּוֹתֶן	סוֹבַבְתֶּן	סוֹבַבְתֶּן	הֲסִבּוֹתֶן	הוּסַבּוֹתֶן	הִסְתּוֹבַבְתֶּן
3c	סָֽבְבוּ	סַ֫בּוּ	נָסַ֫בּוּ	סוֹבְבוּ	סוֹבְבוּ	הֵסֵ֫בּוּ	הוּסַ֫בּוּ	הִסְתּוֹבְבוּ
Imf.1cs.	אָסֹב	אֵסֹב	אֶסַּב	אֲסוֹבֵב	אֲסוֹבַב	אָסֵב	אוּסַב	אֶסְתּוֹבֵב
2m+3f	תָּסֹב	תֵּסֹב	תִּסַּב	תְּסוֹבֵב	תְּסוֹבַב	תָּסֵב	תּוּסַב	תִּסְתּוֹבֵב
2f	תָּסֹ֫בִּי	תֵּסֹ֫בִּי	תִּסַּ֫בִּי	תְּסוֹבְבִי	תְּסוֹבְבִי	תָּסֵ֫בִּי	תּוּסַ֫בִּי	תִּסְתּוֹבְבִי
3m	יָסֹב	יֵסֹב	יִסַּב	יְסוֹבֵב	יְסוֹבַב	יָסֵב	יוּסַב	יִסְתּוֹבֵב
1 c. p.	נָסֹב	נֵסֹב	נִסַּב	נְסוֹבֵב	נְסוֹבַב	נָסֵב	נוּסַב	נִסְתּוֹבֵב
2m	תָּסֹ֫בּוּ	תֵּסֹ֫בּוּ	תִּסַּ֫בּוּ	תְּסוֹבְבוּ	תְּסוֹבְבוּ	תָּסֵ֫בּוּ	תּוּסַ֫בּוּ	תִּסְתּוֹבְבוּ
2f+3f	תְּסֻבֶּ֫ינָה	תְּסֻבֶּ֫ינָה	תִּסַּבֶּ֫ינָה	תְּסוֹבֵבְנָה	תְּסוֹבַבְנָה	תְּסִבֶּ֫ינָה	תּוּסַבֶּ֫ינָה	תִּסְתּוֹבַבְנָה
3m	יָסֹ֫בּוּ	יֵסֹ֫בּוּ	יִסַּ֫בּוּ	יְסוֹבְבוּ	יְסוֹבְבוּ	יָסֵ֫בּוּ	יוּסַ֫בּוּ	יִסְתּוֹבְבוּ
Inf C.	סֹב	סֹב	הִסַּב	סוֹבֵב		הָסֵב		הִסְתּוֹבֵב
Inf A.	סָבוֹב	סֹב	הִסּוֹב	סוֹבֵב	סוֹבַב	הָסֵב		
Imv. ms.	סֹב		הִסַּב	סוֹבֵב	Does	הָסֵב	Does	הִסְתּוֹבֵב
f. sg.	סֹ֫בִּי		הִסָּ֫בִּי	סוֹבְבִי	Not	הָסֵ֫בִּי	Not	הִסְתּוֹבְבִי
m. pl.	סֹ֫בּוּ		הִסַּ֫בּוּ	סוֹבְבוּ	Occur	הָסֵ֫בּוּ	Occur	הִסְתּוֹבְבוּ
f. pl.	סֻבֶּ֫ינָה		הִסַּבֶּ֫ינָה	סוֹבֵבְנָה		הֲסִבֶּ֫ינָה		הִסְתּוֹבַבְנָה
Prt. ms.	סֹבֵב		נָסָב	מְסוֹבֵב	מְסוֹבָב	מֵסֵב	מוּסָב	מִסְתּוֹבֵב
f. sg.	סֹבֶ֫בֶת		נְסַבָּה	מְסוֹבְבָה	מְסוֹבָבָה	מְסִבָּה	מוּסַבָּה	מִסְתַּבֶּ֫בֶת
m. pl.	סֹבְבִים		נְסַבִּים	מְסוֹבְבִים	מְסוֹבָבִים	מְסִבִּים	מוּסַבִּים	מִסְתַּבְּבִים
f. pl.	סֹבְבוֹת		נְסַבּוֹת	מְסוֹבְבוֹת	מְסוֹבָבוֹת	מְסִבּוֹת	מוּסַבּוֹת	מִסְתַּבְּבוֹת

228

HIGH-FREQUENCY PE-NUN VERBS

	נָגַשׁ	נָשָׂא	נָתַן	לָקַח	נָפַל	נָגַד
Qal pf.	נָגַשׁ	נָשָׂא	נָתַן	לָקַה	נָפַל	נָגַד
impf.	יִגַּשׁ	יִשָּׂא	יִתֵּן	יִקַּה	יִפֹּל	Not
imv.	גַּשׁ	שָׂא	תֵּן	קַח	נְפֹל	Used
inf C	גֶּשֶׁת	שְׂאֵת	תֵּת	קַחַת	נְפֹל	
Hiphil pf.	הִגִּישׁ	Rare	Not	Not	הִפִּיל	הִגִּיד
impf.	יַגִּישׁ		Used	Used	יַפִּיל	יַגִּיד
Impf. w. vav-consec.	וַיִּגַּשׁ				וַיִּפֹּל	וַיַּגֵּד
Hophal pf.	Rare	Not	Rare	Rare	Not	הֻגַּד
impf.		Used			Used	יֻגַּד

HIGH-FREQUENCY HOLLOW VERBS

	קָם	שָׁב	מֵת	בָּא	שָׂם	אוֹר
Qal pf.	קָם	שָׁב	מֵת	בָּא	שָׂם	אוֹר
impf.	יָקוּם	יָשׁוּב	יָמוּת	יָבוֹא	יָשִׂים	Rare
jussive	יָקֹם	יָשֹׁב	יָמֹת	יָבֹא	יָשֵׂם	
impf. w. vav-consec.	וַיָּקָם	וַיָּשָׁב	וַיָּמָת	וַיָּבֹא	וַיָּשֶׂם	
ptc. act.	קָם	שָׁב	מֵת	בָּא	שָׂם	אוֹר
Niphal pf.	נָקוֹם	Not	Not	Not	Not	Rare
impf.	יִקוֹם	Used	Used	Used	Used	
Hiphil pf.	הֵקִים	הֵשִׁיב	הֵמִית	הֵבִיא	Rare	הֵאִיר
impf.	יָקִים	יָשִׁיב	יָמִית	יָבִיא		יָאִיר
jussive	יָקֵם	יָשֵׁב	יָמֵת	יָבֵא		יָאֵר
impf. w. vav-consec.	וַיָּקֶם	וַיָּשֶׁב	וַיָּמֶת	וַיָּבֵא		וַיָּאֶר
ptc.	מֵקִים	מֵשִׁיב	מֵמִית	מֵבִיא		מֵאִיר

HIGH-FREQUENCY PE-VAV AND PE-YOD VERBS

Qal pf.	יָלַד	יָשַׁב	יָרַד	הָלַךְ
impf.	יֵלֵד	יֵשֵׁב	יֵרֵד	יֵלֵךְ
impf. w. vav-consec.	וַיֵּלֶד	וַיֵּשֶׁב	וַיֵּרֶד	וַיֵּלֶךְ
imv.	לֵד	שֵׁב	רֵד	לֵךְ
Inf. C	לֶדֶת	שֶׁבֶת	רֶדֶת	לֶכֶת
Hiphil pf.	הוֹלִיד	הוֹשִׁיב	הוֹרִיד	הוֹלִיךְ
impf.	יוֹלִיד	יוֹשִׁיב	יוֹרִיד	יוֹלִיךְ
jussive	יוֹלֵד	יוֹשֵׁב	יוֹרֵד	יוֹלֵךְ
impf. w. vav-consec.	וַיּוֹלֶד	וַיּוֹשֶׁב	וַיּוֹרֶד	וַיּוֹלֶךְ

Qal pf.	יָצָא	יָדַע	יָבֵשׁ	יָרַשׁ
impf.	יֵצֵא	יֵדַע	יִיבַשׁ	יִירַשׁ
impf. w. vav-consec.	וַיֵּצֵא	וַיֵּדַע	וַיִּיבַשׁ	וַיִּירַשׁ
imv.	צֵא	דַּע		רֵשׁ
Inf. C	צֵאת	דַּעַת	יְבֹשֶׁת	רֶשֶׁת
Hiphil pf.	הוֹצִיא	הוֹדִיעַ	Rare	הוֹרִישׁ
impf.	יוֹצִיא	יוֹדִיעַ		יוֹרִישׁ
jussive	יוֹצֵא	יוֹדַע		יוֹרֵשׁ
impf. w. vav-consec.	וַיּוֹצֵא	וַיּוֹדַע		וַיּוֹרֶשׁ

MASTER CHART OF STARTER FORMS OF THE
VARIOUS CLASSES OF HEBREW VERBS

	Strong	Pe-Aleph	Pe-Nun	Pe-Vav	Hollow	Ayin Double	Lamed He
Qal pf.	קָטַל	אָכַל	נָגַשׁ	יָשַׁב	קָט	סַב	גָּלָה
Impf.	יִקְטֹל	יֹאכַל	יִגַּשׁ	יֵשֵׁב	יָקוּם	יָסֹב יִסֹּב	יִגְלֶה
Inf.	קְטֹל	אֲכֹל	גֶּשֶׁת	שֶׁבֶת	קוּם	סֹב	גְּלוֹת
Ptc.	קוֹטֵל	אוֹכֵל	נֹגֵשׁ	יֹשֵׁב	קָם	סוֹבֵב	גֹּלֶה
Niph. pf.	נִקְטַל	נֶאֱכַל	נִגַּשׁ	נוֹשַׁב	נָקוֹם	נָסַב	נִגְלָה
Impf.	יִקָּטֵל	יֵאָכֵל	יִנָּגֵשׁ	יִוָּשֵׁב	יִקּוֹם	יִסַּב	הִגָּלֶה
Imv.	הִקָּטֵל	הֵאָכֵל	הִנָּגֵשׁ	הִוָּשֵׁב	הִקּוֹם	הִסַּב	הִגָּלֵה
Inf.	הִקָּטֵל	הֵאָכֵל	הִנָּגֵשׁ	הִוָּשֵׁב	הִקּוֹם	הִסֵּב	הִגָּלוֹת
Ptc.	נִקְטָל	נֶאֱכָל	נִגָּשׁ	נוֹשָׁב	נָקוֹם	נָסַב	נִגְלֶה
Piel pf.	קִטֵּל	אִכֵּל	נִגֵּשׁ	יִשֵּׁב	קוֹמֵם	סוֹבֵב	גִּלָּה
Impf.	יְקַטֵּל	יְאַכֵּל	יְנַגֵּשׁ	יְיַשֵּׁב	יְקוֹמֵם	יְסוֹבֵב	יְגַלֶּה
Imv.	קַטֵּל	אַכֵּל	נַגֵּשׁ	יַשֵּׁב	קוֹמֵם	סוֹבֵב	גַּלֵּה
Ptc.	מְקַטֵּל	מְאַכֵּל	מְנַגֵּשׁ	מְיַשֵּׁב	מְקוֹמֵם	מְסוֹבֵב	מְגַלֶּה
Pual pf.	קֻטַּל	אֻכַּל	נֻגַּשׁ	יֻשַּׁב	קוֹמַם	סוֹבַב	גֻּלָּה
Impf.	יְקֻטַּל	יְאֻכַּל	יְנֻגַּשׁ	יְיֻשַּׁב	יְקוֹמַם	יְסוֹבַב	יְגֻלֶּה
Imv.							
Ptc.	מְקֻטָּל	מְאֻכָּל	מְנֻגָּשׁ	מְיֻשָּׁב	מְקוֹמָם	מְסוֹבָב	מְגֻלֶּה
Hiphil pf.	הִקְטִיל	הֶאֱכִיל	הִגִּישׁ	הוֹשִׁיב	הֵקִים	הֵסֵב	הִגְלָה
Impf.	יַקְטִיל	יַאֲכִיל	יַגִּישׁ	יוֹשִׁיב	יָקִים	יָסֵב יָסֵב	יַגְלֶה
Imv.	הַקְטֵל	הַאֲכֵל	הַגֵּשׁ	הוֹשֵׁב	הָקֵם	הָסֵב	הַגְלֵה
Ptc.	מַקְטִיל	מַאֲכִיל	מַגִּישׁ	מוֹשִׁיב	מֵקִים	מֵסֵב	מַגְלֶה
Hophal pf.	הָקְטַל	הָאֳכַל	הֻגַּשׁ	הוּשַׁב	הוּקַם	הוּסַב	הָגְלָה
Impf.	יָקְטַל	יָאֳכַל	יֻגַּשׁ	יוּשַׁב	יוּקַם	יוּסַב	יָגְלֶה
Ptc.	מָקְטַל	מָאֳכָל	מֻגָּשׁ	מוּשָׁב	מוּקָם	מוּסָב	מָגְלֶה